Socialism Now

Socialism Now

and other essays

ANTHONY CROSLAND

EDITED BY DICK LEONARD

JONATHAN CAPE

THIRTY BEDFORD SQUARE LONDON

FIRST PUBLISHED 1974
© 1974 BY ANTHONY CROSLAND

JONATHAN CAPE LTD, 30 BEDFORD SQUARE, LONDON W C I

ISBN 0 224 00996 6

PRINTED IN GREAT BRITAIN BY
COX AND WYMAN LTD
LONDON, FAKENHAM AND READING

Contents

Foreword

At first sight this volume may appear to be a natural sequel to two earlier books by Anthony Crosland, *The Future of Socialism* (1956) and *The Conservative Enemy* (1962). Many of the themes discussed in the earlier books are touched upon again here, and in the first essay, in particular, an assessment is made of the extent to which the central conclusions of *The Future of Socialism* still apply nearly twenty years later.

Yet there is an essential and inevitable difference between this book and its two predecessors. When *The Future of Socialism* was published in 1956, the author held no official position in the Labour Party; he was not even in the House of Commons, though he had had five years' previous experience as a Backbench M.P. His influence rested largely on his expertise as a former academic economist.

When he wrote *The Conservative Enemy* his influence was much greater, partly because of the impact of *The Future of Socialism* and partly because, following his return to Parliament in 1959, he had emerged as one of the closest allies of the then party leader, Hugh Gaitskell, and he was widely regarded as a likely candidate for high office.

He was not, however, a Frontbench spokesman for the party, and the major focus of his interests still lay outside the Parliamentary arena. He had the leisure to read widely, and if any particular topic appeared to him significant he was able to immerse himself in it for some time. His writings during this period reflect his varied interests.

After the 1964 General Election his situation underwent a fundamental change. Apart from the first three months, when he served as number two to George Brown, at the Department of Economic Affairs, he held high Cabinet office throughout the whole period of the Labour Government. From 1965 to 1967 he was Secretary of State for Education and Science; from 1967 to 1969 President of the Board of Trade, and from 1969 to 1970 Secretary of State for Local Government and Regional Planning, with a brief to prepare for the merging of several ministries into the Department of the Environment.

Following Labour's electoral defeat, in June 1970, he continued to play a prominent role in the leadership of the Labour Party. He has served for over three years as Shadow Minister for the Environment; he has contested yearly elections to the National Executive Committee of the party; and, in April 1972, he was a candidate for the deputy leadership. There is every reason to believe, that whether Labour is in Government or Opposition, he will remain in an important position within the party.

The change in Crosland's position can be seen in his writing. No longer has he the leisure or the freedom to range as widely as his whim takes him. If he has had new thoughts in recent years about labour relations, penal reform or the role of the mass media, he has had neither the time nor the opportunity to develop them. His intellectual agenda has been dictated, rather, by the treadmill of office–the next departmental meeting, the next Parliamentary speech, the next Standing Committee. The result is apparent in the contents of this book, which primarily represent the subjects which have been of most pressing concern to him as a Minister or an Opposition spokesman.

Though compared with his earlier books his subject-matter is more limited, there are compensating gains, arising from the author's ministerial experience and the greater authority which comes when a man speaks not for himself alone but for a government or a party.

Having been a minister has added an important dimension which his earlier writings lacked. Labour movements, both in Britain and in other countries, have produced a number of brilliant theoreticians who, when given governmental responsibility, were not capable of putting their ideas into practice. Sidney Webb is an obvious example. Yet Crosland was able to reveal his strong practical bent in each of the posts which he held in Harold Wilson's government. Each post wholly absorbed him, which accounts perhaps, in part, for his reputation in Whitehall as one of the strongest Labour ministers, and in each of his departments he was able to combine creative innovation with a high level of administrative skill. He enjoyed the rare satisfaction of the 'ideas man' who is capable of translating his ideas into action. These are, then, the writings of a committed politician, yet one who has not ceased to think deeply and creatively about the problems with which he has been concerned.

The book is divided into five fairly self-contained parts. The first reflects the author's continuing concern about the purposes of Socialism and the role of the Labour Party in contemporary Britain. The title essay was written specifically for this book during the autumn of 1973. The remaining four essays in this section appear in the chronological order in which they were written from 1968 to 1973.

Part Two consists entirely of essays contributed in Opposition, and they arise directly from his Parliamentary activity as housing spokesman. Coming to the subject afresh in 1970, he quickly became immersed in it, and throughout the long and arduous Committee Stage of the Housing Finance Act 1972, he combined astringent criticisms of the Tory Government's proposals with a constant search for radical and relevant solutions which a Labour government could apply. The growing authority with which he has spoken on housing can be gauged by comparing the tentative analysis of the sixth essay with the confident proposals which he advances in the eleventh.

Part Three includes essays or speeches on some of the many problems which are now dealt with by the Department of the Environment, ranging from the third London Airport to the reform of Local Government. This last, which was a speech given on February 18th, 1970, dates from his period as a

Cabinet Minister, as do the three speeches on educational topics, given between January 1966 and June 1967, which comprise Part Four. Part Five, on industrial policy, results from his experience as President of the Board of Trade.

The total time-span over which the essays were written was nearly eight years. No attempt has been made to revise the earlier contributions in the light of subsequent events, and the editing has been confined to the removal of purely topical references; the excision of material which was repetitive because it originally appeared in more than one speech or essay; and a very small number of textual emendations to improve clarity.

For permission to reprint, thanks are due to the Fabian Society and to the various journals in which many of these essays first appeared; they are named at the beginning of each contribution. The author also wishes to thank Mr David Lipsey, for research assistance with a number of the essays, and his former and present secretaries, Mrs Katherine Howes and Mrs Sylvia Boulton, who, together with Mrs Kay Graves, typed–and often retyped–the various chapters of this book.

DICK LEONARD

Part One
Essays on Socialism

1 *Socialism Now*

I wish to discuss firstly whether the revisionist thesis of the 1950s and early 1960s, to which I contributed in *The Future of Socialism* and *The Conservative Enemy*, itself now needs to be drastically revised; and secondly, if not, what this thesis would suggest as the political priorities for the 1970s. To discuss these themes adequately would require the combination of a sabbatical year and a large private think-tank. Being a full-time politician and lacking both of these (though they should ideally be available to politicians in opposition), I approach the task in a tentative mood, wishing that someone better-equipped had undertaken it. For in truth it calls for a major new work of political economy, whereas I can offer only the practical thoughts of a practising and fully-occupied politician.

First, then, where stands the revisionist thesis in the light of the last ten years of experience? There is, at least, no need for revisionists to revise our *definition* of socialism. Socialism, in our view, was basically about equality. By equality, we meant more than a meritocratic society of equal opportunities in which the greatest rewards would go to those with the most fortunate genetic endowment and family background; we adopted the 'strong' definition of equality—what Rawls has subsequently called the 'democratic' as opposed to the 'liberal' conception.[1] We also meant more than a simple (not that it has proved simple in practice) redistribution of income. We wanted a wider social equality embracing also the distribution of property, the educational system, social-class relationships, power and privilege in industry—indeed all that was enshrined in the age-old socialist dream of a more 'classless society'. It seemed to us that the fundamental divide between Left and Right, socialists and non-socialists, had always been about the distribution of wealth, power and class status, and would continue to be so until the economic problem of scarcity disappeared and social relations assumed a utopian character.

This revisionist view of socialism is still, I think, generally accepted in the democratic world. I attended in 1972 a conference in Japan of socialists from virtually every democratic socialist party on 'Socialism in Changing Societies'; the rapporteur reported that 'what they all meant by "socialism" turned out to be a bewildering kaleidoscope of ideas, with "greater equality" and a desire to avoid revolution and maintain a measure of individual freedom as the only common elements.' And in Britain, when non-Marxist critics assess the policies and performance of the Labour Government, they normally apply revisionist criteria and take (apart from the consensus objective of higher living standards) progress towards equality as the yardstick of success or failure.[2]

Of course we can endlessly debate the concept of equality; and there would be many disagreements even amongst socialists. What, for example, are the most crucial causes of inequality—inherited wealth, inherited I.Q., home circumstances, hard work or luck? What are the most important inequalities? Are they of income, capital, education, housing or industrial power? Or are they between the sexes or between races? Or are they perhaps of privacy, sunlight and access to unpolluted beaches? What are the best means of reducing inequality—economic growth, redistribution of income, educational reform or Kennedy-Johnson-style 'Great Society' programmes? What is the trade-off between more equality and faster economic growth? What functional inequalities are necessary in an open industrial society? What constraints on equality are imposed by democratic sentiment and deep-seated notions about 'fair' differentials?

I have not the competence to write a new philosophical treatise on all these matters; nor is it politically necessary. For I observe that there exist extreme inequalities in Britain, which often stem not from hard work but from inheritance and the accident of birth, which are wholly irrelevant to the achievement of economic growth, which are punitive and discriminatory in their effects on the poorer classes and offensive to any canon of social justice. A practising politician in the Britain of the 1970s, not cerebrating in a monastery cell but living day by day in the thick of things, is not required to answer the stern examiner's question: how much equality ultimately? He has plenty of harsh, specific and unmerited inequalities to combat in the next ten years; and a decade is my time-span, not eternity.

But revisionism was a thesis about means as well as ends. It maintained, contrary to traditional Marxist doctrine, that the ownership of the means of production was no longer the key factor which imparted to a society its essential character. Collectivism, private ownership or a mixed economy were all consistent with widely varying degrees not only of equality, but also of freedom, democracy, exploitation, class feeling, elitism, industrial democracy, planning and economic growth. It was therefore possible to achieve the goal of greater equality and other desirable ends within the framework of a mixed economy, with public ownership taking its place as only one of a number of possible means for attaining the ends in view.

The question that arises is whether changes have occurred in the last decade which falsify this thesis, and compel us to alter our views of the route and the methods by which we must seek to achieve our goals.

Important changes have of course occurred on a worldwide scale; the ecological challenge to economic growth, the acceleration of inflation, the energy crisis, the growing discontent with methods of mass production and so on. But I confine my attention to Britain, because the British situation becomes increasingly unique amongst the industrialized countries of the democratic world.

What has changed in Britain? First, there have been six years of Labour Government. It is now the fashion to decry that

Government's performance—to write it off as a total disaster, or at least to exhibit a selective amnesia in which the successes are forgotten and only the failures remembered.

Nobody disputes the central failure of economic policy. In 1970, unemployment was higher, inflation more rapid and economic growth slower, than when the Conservatives left office in 1964. The growth performance in particular was lamentable; G.D.P. in real terms rose by an average of only 2·3 per cent a year compared with 3·8 per cent in the previous six years.[3] Growth was consistently sacrificed to the balance of payments, notably to the defence of a fixed and unrealistic rate of exchange.

This central failure bedevilled all the efforts and good intentions of the Labour Government. It constrained public expenditure. It antagonized the Trade Unions and alienated large groups of workers. It killed the National Plan and frustrated policies for improving the industrial structure (though too much was expected both of indicative planning and industrial policy, which are rather marginal influences on economic performance). And it has made it hard for Labour to claim in future—or, rather, it would have done but for the far worse mess which the Tories are making of the economy—that we can manage things more efficiently than they can.

Yet despite these constraints, solid progress was made on a number of fronts.

Firstly, I take public expenditure, on which so much else depends: income equality (since government benefits are the only effective way of raising the relative incomes of the poorest 20 per cent of the community), standards of health and housing and education, the quality of the environment, and so on. Now it is true that public expenditure as a proportion of G.N.P. was rising in other advanced countries, and moreover that demographic trends would have enforced a substantial increase in Britain between 1964 and 1970.

Yet the actual increase was impressive. A right-wing Government would have used slow growth and a miserable foreign balance as the excuse for a severe austerity in social spending. But the Labour Government, pinioned though it was by constant economic difficulties, raised total public expenditure from 41 per cent to 48 per cent of G.N.P.[4] Education, health and social security benefits all markedly increased their share of the national product; only defence suffered a cut in its share (from 6·7 per cent to 5·7 per cent). The Labour Government has been given insufficient credit for this brave performance – brave because the demands of public expenditure allied to those of the balance of payments left precious little for personal consumption, whose share in final expenditure indeed fell from 55 per cent to 51·8 per cent; and this had serious, perhaps decisive, consequences not only (as I show later) for wage inflation but also for the Government's electoral popularity.

Secondly, the distribution of income. The most dramatic change here was the decrease in the share of profits in G.D.P. (from 15·6 per cent in 1964 to 12·3 per cent in 1970) and increase in the share of wages and salaries (from 67·6 per cent to 70·5 per cent). But this was the result, not of deliberate egalitarian policies, but rather of deflationary pressures, which may well have cost the less well-off more in lost output than they gained from redistribution. One must therefore argue the matter in terms of *personal* incomes.

The final distribution of personal income depends on the distribution of original pre-tax income, the effect of taxes and the effect of benefits. The biggest change under the Labour Government related to benefits. As a result of the large increase in government social expenditure, cash benefits (especially pensions, supplementary benefits and family allowances) rose faster than incomes generally; and their recipients (pensioners, large families and the unemployed) gained more in terms of real disposable income than the rest of the population. There was in addition a high increase in benefits in kind, notably education and health; and this also had a favourable effect.

There is argument about the total effect of the changes which

occurred under the Labour Government. But the most comprehensive study of the subject concludes as follows. 'It would
appear, then, that there was an improvement in the distribution
of income, both vertical and horizontal, under the Labour
Government ... To have promoted a measurable improvement
in the distribution of income against the background of the
deplorably slow rate of growth ... was one of the Labour
Government's main achievements—though, ironically, one
that has received very little recognition from many of Labour's
own supporters.'[5] The Tories, at least, have acknowledged it;
for they have reversed many of the policies which helped to
produce it.

Thirdly, education.[6] Expenditure on education rose from
4·8 per cent of G.N.P. in 1964 to 6·1 per cent in 1970. As a
result, all classes in the community enjoyed significantly more
education than before; and for families with children under
sixteen the effect was strongly redistributive both vertically and
horizontally (i.e. towards larger families).

The huge expansion in the supply of teachers produced a
steady reduction in the pupil-teacher ratio. Standards of school
building and equipment improved in both the primary and
secondary sectors. Circular 10/65 gave a decisive (and in the
long run irreversible) impetus to comprehensive reorganization.
The first, admittedly tentative, steps were taken towards positive discrimination, in favour of those most in need, by the
creation of Educational Priority Areas (as by the Urban Aid
Programme in another sphere). The expansion of higher
education not only far exceeded the Robbins targets; it was also
deliberately biased towards the more flexible and democratically controlled non-university sectors of polytechnics and
colleges of education; and partly as a result of this, working-
class access to higher education showed a small but definite
improvement.

True, the Labour Government never resolved the baffling
dilemma of what priority to give to higher education. For on
the one hand its expansion allows *some* additional working-class

children access to colleges and universities—an important gain. But the middle classes take the preponderance of extra places (in Communist as much as in Western countries[7]); and in this sense the more that is spent on higher education, the more the poor are subsidizing the rich who benefit most from it. Neither, despite the Newsom Commission, did they solve the problem of the public schools. But the achievement was substantial; and the best evidence again is the determination of Tory Ministers to reverse so many of the policies.

Fourthly, housing. This was without doubt one of the top priorities, and a flurry of activity, circulars and Parliamentary Bills characterized the whole six years. But reviewing it with hindsight, the performance was typical of so much of what the Labour Government did. On the one hand, many admirable individual things were done, some with consensus ends but others with egalitarian ends in mind: protection for the private tenant, higher subsidies to local authorities, leasehold enfranchisement, the option mortgage scheme, the impetus to rehabilitation under the 1969 Act, and so on. And more new houses were built than ever before in a comparable period—25 per cent more than the Conservatives built in the preceding six years; though the target of 500,000 houses a year, which had been so rashly set, was not achieved.

Yet there was little sign of a coherent, overall egalitarian strategy. In 1970, as I show in later chapters, the system of housing finance was still riddled with anomalies and inequalities, both within the three sectors (owner-occupier, municipal and private rented) and between them. The greatest help did not go to either the households or the areas most in need; too much tax relief went to those least in need; and no satisfactory solution was found to the problem of land values. Moreover the house-building programme, doggedly protected from attack during the first four difficult years, was finally a casualty (along with other programmes such as the raising of the school-leaving age) of the post-devaluation retrenchment. Much that was beneficial was accomplished, and the record

was far from disgraceful (as one can easily see by comparing it
with the subsequent record of 1970–74). But it would have
been much better for a more systematic egalitarian strategy.

Regional policy, on the other hand, *was* systematically
thought out; and many of Labour's innovations—the creation
of Development Areas, differential investment grants, the
Regional Employment Premium, the later gradation of Special
Development and Intermediate Areas—were ingenious and
imaginative. These measures had to struggle against a continuing loss of jobs in the declining basic industries (coal, agriculture, railways, textiles, steel, ports and shipbuilding) which were
so heavily concentrated in the problem areas—a loss far larger
than had occurred in the previous six years. But regional
policies diverted a net 220,000 jobs to the hard-pressed areas, as
well as helping both total output and the balance of payments.[8]
Unemployment in the Development Areas, as a multiple of
unemployment in the country as a whole, fell from 2·21 in
1964 to 1·67 in 1970;[9] and the basis had been laid for a
genuine economic take-off in the regions.

Important reforms were implemented in other fields: the
reorganization of government in 1969/70 for the first systematic
attack on environmental pollution; the impetus to regional
land-use planning; the strong encouragement to the conservation of both historic cities and the countryside; the fateful
decision to withdraw from East of Suez and so finally abandon
an outmoded imperial role; the many libertarian reforms
helped on to the statute book by an enlightened Home Secretary;
and so on.

So much was done of genuine and lasting value; and the
achievement looks still better from the perspective of four years
of subsequent Tory rule. Labour policies on taxation, comprehensive education, rents and social benefits must have meant
something for equality if the Tories are so anxious to reverse
them. And when one notes the dissatisfaction with the record,
especially amongst social workers, one must always remember
that a modern welfare state, by continuously raising its stan-

dards, ensures that it always falls short of its own expectations. It thus breeds a permanent state of dissatisfaction, which provides ammunition for those who want to argue that the whole approach has failed.

Yet the performance (and I must take my share of responsibility) did not live up to the hopes which we, in the Government, had entertained. For myself, I become most vividly aware of this when I recall the many proposals in *The Future of Socialism* and *The Conservative Enemy*, some of which appeared at various times in Labour manifestoes, which were not put into effect: for example, a wealth tax, a tax on gifts and higher death duties graded according to size of bequest; the public ownership of land and the municipalization of private rented housing; the integration of the public schools (though I know the difficulties only too well!); a full-scale national superannuation scheme; the nationalization of industrial assurance; a state holding company, a government unit trust, and an active policy of competitive public enterprise; a tax on advertising; a fourth educational T.V. channel; and so on.

These were specific failures. The more general disappointment has been that the pressure of democracy has exerted much less beneficial influence than I anticipated, so that even after six years of Labour rule, Britain in the 1970s is conspicuous for its persistent and glaring class inequalities, which an appallingly weak economy makes it hard to tackle.

We retain an amazing sense of class and little sense of community. Company chairmen pay themselves huge salary increases at a time of wage restraint; trade union leaders and local councillors debate whether to defy the law; both are a tiny minority, yet they each symbolize the lack of respect for community decisions. Class divisions are perpetuated by the existence of a privileged and segregated sector of education to which better-off parents automatically send their children. The distribution of wealth is grossly unequal; and although this is largely the result of inheritance, huge fortunes are still being

made (and at a wicked social cost) in land and property specula-
tion—indeed these fortunes, along with scandals such as
Lonrho, have given the last decade its unpleasantly mercenary
flavour. Meanwhile a stubborn residue of poverty persists,
notably amongst the old, the sick and the disabled, but also
amongst low-paid workers.

The housing situation has deteriorated in the last three years,
and homelessness is on the increase. The environmental crisis
of the inner cities, affecting the poor much more than the rich,
continues unabated. In spite of the strength of the unions,
workers in industry (even the so-called 'affluent' workers)
remain subordinate and inferior in terms not only of income,
but also of status, fringe benefits and job security. The labour
issue continues to dominate our society, and class relations in
industry are characterized by a mutual distrust amounting
often to open warfare.

A general malaise shows up also in political attitudes. The
proportion of people voting in British general elections has
steadily declined since the Second World War; this is true of
no other Western democracy for which reliable data are available. The turn-out at the 1970 General Election was the lowest
since 1945, and lower than in nearly every other comparable
democracy.[10]

At the same time our economic performance has continued
to worsen as compared with other advanced nations. If one
extrapolates recent growth-rates, one finds that by 1985 G.N.P.
per head in Britain will be only half that of France and Germany; indeed, it will be one of the lowest in Europe. True,
international comparisons of standards of living are fraught
with statistical difficulties; and in any case extrapolation is not
prophecy. But the underlying trend is not in dispute.

Slow growth has already exacted a heavy toll. Working-
class living standards are lower than they should be. Public
expenditure is continually subject to painful crisis cuts. There
is never enough money for all sorts of excellent purposes, not
only in the social policy field but for the arts, science, sport and

recreation. There is a constant scrimping and saving; and in the quality and quantity of our social and cultural provision Britain has fallen badly behind Scandinavia and Western Europe.

This dismal record creates a public mood of discord and discontent, the more so since the 1950s and early 1960s had witnessed an exceptionally rapid rise in living standards, which indeed evoked the phrase 'the revolution of rising expectations'. But these expectations were not fulfilled in the later 1960s. Taking four-year periods from 1948 to 1968, the annual compound rate of growth of net real income of male manual workers moved as follows: 0·7 per cent (1948–52), 3·5 per cent (1952–6), 2·1 per cent (1956–60), 1·3 per cent (1960–64), 0·5 per cent (1964–8); there was then some rise in the following years.[11] The annual growth-rate of consumers' expenditure in real terms moved as follows: 2·8 per cent in 1955–60, 2·7 per cent in 1960–65 and only 1·5 per cent in 1966–70.

The decline in the late 1960s had a number of causes: the slow-down in the overall rate of growth, the need to transfer resources to exports and the Labour Government's laudable determination to increase public expenditure. But it manifested itself in a painful way. For the first time, the mass of manual workers found themselves caught in the net of progressive direct taxation. In the 1950s the typical manual worker paid virtually no income tax; even in 1960 his tax and insurance contributions took only 8 per cent of his earnings; but by 1970 they took nearly 20 per cent.[12] Moreover, since under a progressive tax system marginal rates of tax are higher than the average rate, a large segment of any increase in income went to the Exchequer; and ever-bigger increases in *money* wages were required to maintain the accustomed rise in net *real* wages. The increase in wage-taxation also created a growing distortion of traditional differentials. The inevitable result (exacerbated by successive attempts to impose industrial relations legislation) was more inflation, strikes and industrial unrest as workers sought to restore both previous levels of general real net earnings and previous differentials.

The lessons of this experience are not entirely palatable. They underline the conclusion of a later chapter. Socialism and equality require a relative transfer of resources from private consumption to public expenditure; economic exigencies may demand a further transfer to higher exports or investment. But under conditions of slow growth, efforts to achieve these transfers inevitably provoke inflation. For since they cannot come from the fruits of rapid growth, they must come from higher taxation of existing incomes. But higher indirect taxes put up prices; higher direct taxes provoke compensating claims for higher money wages and salaries. In our slow-growth economy the shift of resources away from personal consumption has harshly exacerbated the problem of inflation.

There is no brushing aside the evils of inflation. It redistributes income from the poor to the rich—from welfare claimants, the lower-paid and the worst-organized to the well-organized, strong professional groups and owners of real property. It jeopardizes full employment. It stampedes Governments, which naturally fear its electoral consequences, into precipitate and damaging actions. It engenders a pervasive mood of watchful envy and insecurity about the future, and incites a destructive competitive struggle between organized groups to protect their own living standards. All these features are disturbingly prevalent in British society in the 1970s.

So extreme class inequalities remain, poverty is far from eliminated, the economy is in a state of semi-permanent crisis and inflation is rampant. All this undoubtedly belies the relative optimism of *The Future of Socialism* (though not the more pessimistic tone of *The Conservative Enemy*). Do these setbacks to our hopes demonstrate that the revisionist analysis of means and ends was wrong, and the Marxist analysis which it sought to rebut was right?

There has indeed been a revival of semi-Marxist thought in Britain; and naturally it strongly maintains this view, asserting that a new and sinister crisis of capitalism is upon us, which can be resolved only by a massive programme of public ownership.

Outside fringe and sectarian groups (and possibly the French Socialist Party), this revival (and generally the ideological dispute about nationalization) seems to be largely confined to Britain; and perhaps this is hardly surprising. For if one examines the Western world as a whole there are no clear signs of a new and fundamental crisis. Certainly there are periodic monetary crises and a growing problem of inflation; and the West has now to adjust to temporarily scarce and permanently more expensive energy. Yet full employment is generally maintained; economic growth continues; world trade expands; and the technological and growth gap between the Western and the Communist publicly owned economies is actually widening. The living standards and horizons of ordinary people in the West have dramatically expanded in the last two decades; and though the short-term outlook (as I write) is grim, and growth may be slower in future, no long-term crisis comparable to that of the 1930s seems imminent.

There is, however, one possible exception to this generalization — Great Britain, for all the reasons given in the previous section. This is indeed a matter for the most searching and anxious analysis; for the depressing facts are not in dispute. The question is: does it support the new Marxist thesis?

According to this thesis, a major transformation of power-relationships has taken place in the British economy, due partly to the growing concentration of industry and partly to the growth of the multi-nationals. Economic power has moved sharply away from the state and the workers, towards a small oligarchy of private manufacturing firms. These firms were easily able to frustrate the efforts of the last Labour Government to create or induce greater equality, faster growth, higher investment and exports, regional justice, price and profit restraint and industrial democracy.

Thus it is capitalist power which is, in the last resort, the cause both of the inequalities and the poor performance described above. The ownership of the means of production is ever more obviously the dominant influence on society; the revisionist thesis to the contrary has been disproved. It follows that a massive increase in public ownership is required, not so much for reasons specific to any particular firm or industry, but generally to transfer this concentrated power and wealth from a small economic oligarchy to the people.

I shall deal in turn with the questions of power, equality, economic performance and the social conduct of private industry.

First, then, power. It is quite correct that concentration in manufacturing industry has greatly increased in Britain since about 1950; indeed the Labour Government itself accelerated the process by its penchant for industrial restructuring. The largest hundred manufacturing enterprises produced 46 per cent of net manufacturing output in 1970 compared with only 21 per cent in 1949.[13]

Has this led to a major increase in the power of private industry relative to that of the state, the trade unions and the community generally? It seems an implausible thesis in the light of other trends in evidence during the same period.

As to the state, total public expenditure rose between 1964 and 1972 from 41 per cent to 49 per cent of G.N.P.; and total public investment, which of course embraces all the really large projects such as Maplin, Concorde and (effectively) the Channel Tunnel, now amounts to 41 per cent of domestic fixed capital formation. The state-owned industrial sector was enlarged by the take-over of steel and the expansion of the existing nationalized industries; in 1972 investment by the nationalized sector was equal to 42 per cent of all private investment in the company sector and 83 per cent of private manufacturing investment. The Labour Government passed a mass of new legislation controlling and limiting the acti-vities of private firms—on prices, corporate taxation, factory and office location, pollution, trade descriptions, redundancy payments, and so on indefinitely. The economy became even more a managed one (as any economy will increasingly be, which pursues, apart from anything else, policies for prices and incomes, the distribution of industry, the control of pollution and, in the near future, the conservation of energy supplies); and the freedom of the private firm was more and more circumscribed by both the macro- and the micro-economic policies of government.

No one has argued, so far as I am aware, that the power of the trade unions diminished during this period, though they naturally feel resentful at their failure (for the reasons explained above) to achieve real gains in living standards. They wholly defeated the Labour Government, and effectively frustrated the Tory Government, in major confrontations over industrial relations legislation; while the miners and others, in an open battle over wages in 1972, forced Mr Heath into a humiliating reversal of his chosen economic policies. Some of the commanding heights of the economy are now to be found in union headquarters in Euston Road (though the dominant heights are for the present in the capitals of Saudi Arabia and Kuwait).

At the same time, British manufacturing industry has felt an unpleasantly cold blast from a number of different directions. While the degree of concentration has increased, so has competition (as the British motor, aero-engine, electrical equipment and other industries know to their cost). The rate of introduction of close substitutes for existing products has never been higher; and recent years have witnessed a dramatic growth in manufactured imports. Between 1966 and 1972 imports of final manufactures into Britain trebled in value; the value of home manufacturing output rose by only 55 per cent.

Due partly to increased competition and partly to the combination of wage pressure and economic stagnation, profits fell sharply during this period. Indeed Messrs Glyn and Sutcliffe, asserting that the share of profits halved between 1964 and 1970, conclude that British capitalism 'is now literally fighting for survival.'[14] Other economists take a less dramatic view, but none disputes that the pre-tax rate of profit slumped badly in the late 1960s. Whether desirable or not in the national or working-class interest, this hardly suggests a business class capable of enforcing its will on a Labour Government.

Whatever the future of profits, another trend seems firmly established in all advanced countries: a steady shift of the labour force out of manufacturing (and agriculture) into services (trade, finance, transport, health, recreation, research, education and government). In the United States the service sector now accounts for more than half of both total employment and G.N.P.; and the fastest-growing industries are the public sector industries of central and local government and the education service.[15] The trend was briefly halted in Britain by the introduction of S.E.T. Yet even so, manufacturing employment had fallen by 1971 to 38 per cent of all employment; manufacturing output was some £16,000 millions compared with a G.N.P. of over £48,000 millions; and the share of the hundred largest manufacturing companies in G.N.P. was 15 per cent (and so that of a sample twenty-five of them would be under 4 per cent). This hardly seems an overwhelming share.

Thus manufacturing industry, with falling or stagnant profits, severe competition from imports and a declining share of total employment, is faced by ever-increasing state activity (in terms of both expenditure and direct regulation), a trade union movement capable of blowing even governments off-course and (in addition) a growing consumer and environmental lobby. The power-game does not seem so one-sided after all.

But what of the multinationals, which are said to be insidiously undermining the sovereignty of national governments? Fortunately, there are now two up-to-date and authoritative reports on this subject; both display a clear scepticism towards the more lurid fears which have been expressed about national enslavement to international capital.[16]

When one speaks of multinationals one is simply talking of direct overseas investment by (mainly) manufacturing companies. The extent of foreign direct investment in Britain (which was generally encouraged, incidentally, by the Labour Government) is as follows. Including oil, overseas interests accounted in 1968 for about 14 per cent of the net assets of all United Kingdom manufacturing companies and 11 per cent of all United Kingdom assets. The proportion was growing quite rapidly throughout the 1960s. The preponderant element in foreign ownership is American.[17]

The instinctive reaction is natural enough.

Simple nationalistic sentiments and fear of large organizations generally are enough to induce a presumption that the growth of multinational enterprise poses some kind of threat. But these vague feelings, however strongly held, are not specific enough either to establish that in fact a danger exists, or to indicate appropriate responses on the part of host-country governments. To do that, careful investigation is required.

Such investigation shows that the effect of foreign investment on the balance of payments is 'generally favourable'. There is neither gain nor loss to research and technology; in any case, the 'view that an independent technology is essential to our prosperity and the avoidance of American domination is romantic nonsense'. The potential gain to regional policy from foreign subsidiaries is 'quite great'; their location pattern 'does not differ substantially from that of British industry as a whole'. They do not 'worsen the competitive position compared to what would be the case if the direct investment was not there'. Summing up, inward investment has increased real income by some 2 per cent (far more, for example, than any possible gain from joining the Common Market).

But the fear still remains that the power of multi-nationals to switch investment from one country to another—from Dagenham to Dusseldorf—threatens our national sovereignty; and American-owned car firms periodically make noises which seem to confirm this fear. In fact it normally appears to be bargaining bluff; moreover trade unions are becoming better organized internationally to call the bluff. And to the extent to which it is real, the threat to move operations to a foreign country would exist (especially inside the Common Market) equally with a British-owned firm; indeed, 'the fact that the foreign firm is foreign, is here on sufferance, and the possibility of exchange control tend, under present conditions at least, to make it more publicly accountable than domestic firms'. Professor Steuer and his colleagues conclude that, 'our search for concrete cases of loss of national autonomy through inward investment produced very little ... We find hardly any grounds for believing in a serious loss of national autonomy.'

There are of course potential dangers—to the balance of payments from leads and lags, or to tax revenue from the fiddling of transfer prices (though it is hard to imagine that they could conceivably offset a 2 per cent gain in national income); and more urgent dangers are only too real (as the behaviour of I.T.T. in Chile showed) in the case of the less developed countries. Moreover political considerations must set an upper limit on the foreign ownership of domestic assets. The position needs to be continuously monitored and government powers need to be robustly used—to legislate, to tax, to police, to embargo—on both the national and international level. And if there are no other means of controlling the activity of a foreign subsidiary, it can always be nationalized.

Yet the multinational trend may have passed its peak. American foreign investment, which has been the main contributory factor, may become less attractive in future as European labour costs approach American levels and the U.S. regains competitiveness in manufacturing industries. And political influences have moved heavily against the foreign-controlled corporation; the trend is now everywhere towards joint ventures, minority shareholdings and even management contracts without any shareholding. As the U.N. Report puts it:

The increasing power of host governments individually or
as members of a regional group to insist on participation,
if not outright control, the growing sentiment in some
home countries for stricter scrutiny of multinational
corporations, and the fact that first tentative steps towards
some form of international action have been taken, suggest
that the days are gone when it could be predicted with some
justification that the world economy would eventually be
dominated by a handful of giant firms.[18]

It is therefore hard to discern a massive shift of power to the
private corporation; nor is any concrete evidence for it ever
advanced. One can hardly adduce the inadequate levels of
investment or exports under the Labour Government since
these stemmed mainly from the failure of government *macro-
economic* policies; they were not paralleled in other mixed
economies of the Western world. Nor can one blame private
enterprise for not introducing industrial democracy, when the
government was not urging it to do so, and the nationalized
sector itself was making only the most minimal efforts in this
direction. As to regional policy, which is so often mentioned,
it has never been demonstrated that the large corporations
regularly flouted or ignored the government's distribution of
industry policies, or that a more rigidly *dirigiste* policy (if
indeed it were possible, which it has not proved to be with
existing nationalized industries) would have produced better
results than the actual policies of the Labour Government.

So I do not detect a drastic transformation of power relationships. Economically, British manufacturing industry took a
rough buffeting in the 1960s. Politically, it allowed itself to be
pilloried for a poor performance which was at least equally the
fault of government. In terms of personal wealth and profit it
came a very poor second-best to the worlds of property and
finance; and its influence and prestige (relative, for example, to
that of the mercantile tradition of the City) are less than in any
other advanced Western country.

c

Certainly the process of mergers and concentration has gone too far from many points of view (including efficiency); what is needed is, at the least, a much firmer competition policy to halt it,[19] and ideally a policy of enforced divestment to reverse it. But the process has probably made government control easier, not harder; and I see no reason to alter the revisionist thesis that government can generally impose its will (provided it has one) on the private corporation.

In any case, would power relationships change dramatically if the large corporations were all to be nationalized? If one imagines the hundred largest private firms in public ownership —what would be the effect on the distribution of power? Here I return to Weber, who is often more relevant to our current problems than Marx. He predicted that control of state enterprises would end up in the hands of a managerial bureaucracy, just as removed as the private corporation, both from dictation by the government and solidarity with the workers. And so, surely, it has often proved to be. There are splendid exceptions which provide a showpiece for public enterprise. But British Rail, the B.B.C., the gas and electricity boards are precisely described as 'managerial bureaucracies'.

This raises a problem which goes far beyond the field of industry. As the area of state intervention widens, so the difficulty of effective control from Westminster and Whitehall increases; hence the constant pressure to create new semi-autonomous bureaucratic institutions—planning councils, health and water authorities, research institutes, new agencies of every kind—which are not properly accountable to any elected body. And many of the new industrial policies promoted in the name of socialism tend always to a bureaucratic elitism on the French model.

Now some of this is inevitable; bureaucratic rules are necessary in an increasingly complex society. But one must not confuse it with socialism, or assume that more state power automatically brings greater democratic accountability in its train. Certainly the present state industries are not adequately accountable or responsible. True, government is generally able to impose its will on them (as on private industries).[20] But there is little democratic responsibility or popular control; nor, as they are currently managed, are they markedly more sensitive to the wishes of consumers than (say) I.C.I. or Unilever. Such at least is the overwhelming view of the public, who indeed believe that the ordinary person has *less and less* influence on the way these industries are run.[21]

Let us hope that this will change in the future; here is a fruitful field for exciting experiment in the existing public sector. But the voters will wish to see the colour of the Labour Party's money. If nationalization is to represent not simply a change from a remote private to a remote public bureaucracy, but a genuine transfer of power to the community, the consumers and the workers, they must produce evidence to show that this will actually occur; at the least, they must be seen to be making the attempt in the industries which are already state owned.

I turn from power to equality, and ask whether the relationship between equality and public ownership has altered in the last decade. I am concerned here mainly with the unequal distribution (and especially inheritance) of private property, which is at the heart of the class system; and with the contribution which public ownership can make to redistributing it.

It is now generally recognized that nationalization with fair compensation has little effect on *existing* wealth-distribution; the former shareholders, now holding government stock, are as rich as they were before. Nor will it have much effect, even in the long run, unless the nationalized industries make adequate profits; for otherwise they must borrow from the private sector to finance their expansion, and private wealth will grow *pari passu* with publicly owned assets. These two considerations explain why post-war nationalization in Britain has had no visible influence on the distribution of wealth; stiff taxes on property and land would have had far more.

But public ownership, *provided that it is accompanied by public saving*, can make a significant contribution in the long term. It is a means, not of redistributing existing wealth (which can only be done by taxation), but of collecting for the community the increase in wealth which flows from economic expansion.

This purpose will occasionally be served by the public ownership and management of entire industries where these are exceptionally profitable; the most obvious example is development land. But generally the concern here is simply with the ownership of property, not with its management or control. This is an important distinction. Where the concern is with inefficient management or inadequate public control, then we must acquire the entire assets of a *particular* firm or industry by the legal act of nationalization. But this is not the sensible way to proceed where the object is *generally* to increase the public ownership of profitable assets. It is slow; even if we nationalize the twenty-five largest companies we should be acquiring only a small fraction of total private property (much of it belonging to pension and insurance funds). It raises acute problems of the supply of top management. Some of the industries to be taken over would turn out to be loss-makers rather than profit-makers; and where they were efficient profit-makers a mass take-over would be hard to justify to the public. The take-over of individual enterprises must be justified on other grounds; this I do in the next section.

From the point of view of equality the object would be to use public savings to finance economic expansion; and the way to do this is through the government acquisition of shares on a wide front. This raises no problems of management or control; indeed it could 'be combined with private management, or worker management, or consumer management, or state management, or any other industrial form, without violating the socialist concern to restrain the growth of private wealth'.[22] I and others have, in the past, suggested many ways in which the government could use public savings to purchase shares— through a death-duty capital fund, a state investment trust, and so on; we lost the best of all opportunities when we failed to

establish ten years ago a large National Superannuation Fund
with the power to invest in equities. I return later to the question
of what methods should be utilized now.

I turn next to the relationship between industrial ownership
and economic performance.

There are two separate issues here. The first is the poor
growth-rate, so much lower than in the 1950s, of the years
1964–70. Now it is hard to attribute this primarily to a failure
on the part of private industry. For the evidence suggests that
the productivity of private manufacturing industry has improved considerably over the last ten years[23] (though that
still does not make it particularly marvellous by international
standards). The reason why the economy did not grow up to
the limit of this higher productive potential was that the final
demand was not there. This had nothing to do with too much or
too little socialism; it was due to the deflationary policies which
stemmed inexorably from the Labour Government's obsession
with a particular parity for sterling. Thus the Labour Government's overall economic failure sheds no light on the rights and
wrongs of alternative socialist theories.

Yet there has been a change, and a most welcome one, during
the last decade. When I wrote *The Future of Socialism*, the
nationalized industries were for the most part demonstrably
less efficient than private industries. But in the second decade
of their existence, having got over their teething troubles, they
have displayed an exceptionally rapid rise in productivity.
During this latter period, 'the public enterprise sector has had
a significantly better performance in respect of technical
efficiency than the private sector ... The nationalized industries
must, on the whole, be judged an economic success, and it
seems likely that they have had a favourable impact on the
national welfare.' So writes the author of the most exhaustive
study of this question yet undertaken.[24]

True, there is controversy about the reasons for the improvement, and some doubt as to whether the trend has continued

into the 1970s; and there are glaring exceptions such as British
Rail and the Post Office. But there clearly has been a change for
the better, and it is reflected in an altered climate of public
opinion. Moreover, at the same time as public enterprise has
become more efficient, Rolls-Royce and Upper Clyde Ship-
builders have come to symbolize the decline of private enterprise. This may or may not be fair. Nevertheless the demise of
such famous firms illustrates the fact that it is now absurd to
generalize about public industries being *ipso facto* less (or more)
efficient than private industries. In our future policies we
can take a wholly pragmatic view and treat each case on its
merits.

Thus, although I personally have no great love for the idea
of yet more state monopolies, one can readily accept the case
for nationalizing certain industries where structural or management changes are needed that cannot be achieved without
unified ownership, or which for social reasons (for example,
regional policy or external social economics) need to be run
at a loss.

One can still more readily adopt (or in my case re-adopt, for I
supported the idea twenty years ago) an active policy of
competitive public enterprise: that is, the establishment (either
from scratch or by take-over) of state companies or joint
ventures to compete with private enterprise—to act as highly
competitive price-leaders and pace-setters, provide a yardstick
for efficiency, support the government's investment plans, and
above all produce a better product or service. A number of
British industries cry out for aggressive public competition—
for example, construction, machine-tools, pharmaceuticals, the
insurance companies and the building societies.

These public enterprises would be controlled by a State
Holding Company. But it would also be necessary to have a
State Investment Bank (perhaps based on the recently-amalga-
mated F.C.I. and I.C.F.C.) with a far-ranging entrepreneurial
role—Part I.R.C., part government merchant bank, it would
have the power and finance to strengthen competition, rede-

ploy management, back sensible but risky investment projects, restructure industry (though hopefully with a due scepticism about the advantages of size) and advise on the inevitable periodic rescue operations (perhaps in the motor industry next?). In Mr Dell's words, it would be 'the responsible agency for the conduct of selective intervention'; its task would be to inject the public interest into industrial situations.

This is a fresher and more attractive approach than the old one. It moves away from monolithic industry nationalization towards nationalization by *company*. It thus gives government a lever for improving standards without destroying consumer choice or creating unresponsive leviathans. The concept of a mixed economy has not been sufficiently understood in the past. It should not necessarily be an economy in which whole sectors are privately and whole sectors publicly owned. It should be a *genuinely* mixed economy, based on a variety of ownership forms and social controls designed to provide the best possible blend of social efficiency, growth and choice.

One should not expect too much from either more intervention or more nationalization. Little was left by 1970 of the glowing 1964 themes of industrial restructuring and technological revolution; vast sums were wasted on the aerospace industry, while nothing effective was done for industries (such as machine-tools or construction) which desperately needed an active policy. Governments do not always see the public interest so much more clearly than private firms.

As to public enterprise, the right balance has not yet been found between Ministerial control and entrepreneurial freedom—between on the one hand excessive mucking about (such as occurred in 1970-71) and on the other the creation of non-accountable state bureaucracies. There is still disagreement about pricing policy, financial targets and the responsibility for non-commercial social ventures. Above all there is often a basic ambivalence on the question of profit. The N.E.B., proposed in Labour's programme, is to be a profit-making enterprise, yet it is to undertake investments which private enterprise finds unprofitable; and both it and the state monopolies, while being, in theory, enjoined to make profits and not rely on government subsidies, are certain in practice to bear the brunt (as they have done under the Tories) of any prices and incomes policy. This is why the contribution of nationalization to the redistribution of wealth should not be over-estimated; it is also what bedevils attempts to improve industrial relations in the state sector.

State Holding Companies and acts of nationalization in other countries have proved a useful weapon in a mix of policies designed to overcome some of the more objectionable features of the modern economy; and so they will prove in Britain. But one must not expect them to revolutionize society.

I turn to the social behaviour of industry and its relationship to ownership. Probably the changing climate of opinion and the deteriorating image of private enterprise, to which I referred above, owes less to the economic performance than to the recent *social* behaviour of some private firms—behaviour which led even Mr Heath to speak of 'the unpleasant and unacceptable face of capitalism'.

Recent years have produced a spate of disagreeable scandals in the private sector: the corporate meanness of Distillers' over the thalidomide children, the inflexible profit-maximization of Roche Products in respect of Health Service drugs, the quick fortunes made out of the nation's land and housing needs, the assertion by a handful of company chairmen of their sole duty to shareholders, even at a time of income restraint, and the avarice, cupidity and lack of patriotism of the Lonhro directors.

Although such squalid behaviour is the exception rather than the rule, it has combined with other factors (slow growth, statutory price and profit control, the collapse of certain famous firms, the disastrous failure and subsequent abandonment of Mr Heath's abrasive pro-capitalist policies) to induce a deep unease and defensive uncertainty in the ranks of private industry. With shareholder democracy no longer a reality, big business displays a growing concern about its legitimacy, the proper locus of responsibility and the role of profit. The C.B.I. argues that business must act as 'a good citizen' and develop a 'new ethical dimension';[25] the British Institute of Management publishes a book giving businessmen practical advice on how to draw up a social responsibility audit;[26] the talk is once again of government directors, consumer directors, two-tier boards of management, codes of professional conduct and the rest.

I have discussed these questions in previous books and always come to the same conclusion. With the managerial revolution, there *is* a vacuum in accountability and a loss (in some sense) of legitimacy.

> The decisions of the corporation are legitimized neither by the 'rights of property' (as they might have been under Lockean capitalism), nor by consumer sovereignty (as they might be if we had perfect competition and profit-maximization), nor by any public accountability. They are taken by self-perpetuating managerial oligarchies responsible to no one. These oligarchies ... increasingly see themselves as quasi-public trustees for the general welfare;[27]

and they construct their own definitions of where that welfare lies.

But to whom *should* they be accountable? For they have, most of us would think, a diverse set of responsibilities: to workers, customers, consumers, shareholders, the localities in which they operate and the whole community represented by the state. None of these groups can or should enjoy an undivided right of control; and they are too numerous and diverse (and their interests too conflicting) for them all to be represented on the board of management or to have their 'rights' codified and enshrined in an Act of Parliament.

It is easy to become bemused by constitution-making and

elaborate talk of legitimacy and accountability. (Have not the
Church of England, the M.C.C. and Shelter, with no private
investors, shown themselves just as much non-accountable
and self-perpetuating oligarchies as I.C.I.?) The real questions
are the wealth, the power and the social behaviour of the
private firm. These are matters of acute public interest and
concern. This concern should not be expressed by devising
new theories of legitimacy or ingenious constitutions. It should
be expressed partly through the countervailing power of
workers, consumers and local authorities, but primarily through
government action. It is the direct responsibility of the democratic state, as guardian of the public welfare, to lay down the
detailed ground rules and compel the private (and the nationalized) firm to conform to its own positive views of where the
public interest lies.

This it will do by legislation, taxation and controls. But a
condition of effective action on the *social* aspects of company
behaviour is that much more should be known about how
companies actually behave. Hence the importance of the
proposal that the Companies Acts should be drastically revised
not only to outlaw present company malpractices, but also to
require an annual 'social audit' as well as the financial balance-
sheet—an audit that would cover health and safety (as the
Robens Committee recommended), the employment of elderly
and disabled workers, reports of independent consumer
testing, levels of pollution by noise, emissions and effluents,
and so on.

In the last resort governments can always nationalize. But
they should not take the easy way out of assuming that public
bodies are always beyond reproach. Not all nationalized
industries have flawless records on safety, the control of
pollution or even incorruptibility. The British Government is
itself the largest single employer of low-wage workers; and it
treated the Mersey Docks stockholders in the most scandalous
fashion. Experience has shown that the mere fact of public
responsibility does not immunize the state against the age-old

instincts of greed and personal gain. We in Britain, after some of the recent events in local government, should be properly modest in this matter; elected office-holders in the United States have not recently shown themselves to be paragons of rectitude; and the continuing black-market and embezzlement cases in the Communist countries, punished often by death, show only too sadly that the problem here is not simply one of capitalism but of universal human behaviour.

Having examined in turn the relationship of ownership to power, equality, economic performance and social behaviour, I see no reason to abandon the revisionist analysis of socialism in favour of a refurbished Marxism. Developments in Britain during the last decade have been acutely disappointing to a democratic socialist, but the explanation does not appear to lie primarily in the British pattern of ownership. Other countries with a similar pattern have moved ahead much faster; and no evidence has been presented to show how or why, in Britain alone, a massive transfer of ownership is either necessary to achieving our goals or would in fact help to achieve them.

So public ownership remains (along with taxation, legislation, government controls, trade union action and so on) one of a number of means to achieving our socialist ends—and a means which, in the light of the improved performance of the public sector, can now be used more freely. My own priorities for public ownership would be land (overwhelmingly first), private rented housing, parts of both the construction and insurance industries, and the creation of a state oil company to operate in the North Sea and elsewhere around our shores (as part of a policy for securing national control over, and maximum benefit from, these vital new energy resources). I think these would make the most direct contribution to a better distribution of wealth, power and welfare. But a sound empirical case can be made out for the other ownership proposals in Labour's current programme; though I doubt if they could all be carried through in a single Parliament, and in any case one should not, in the light of the still unsolved problems of the existing public sector, raise expectations of miracles to follow.

British society—slow-moving, rigid, class-ridden—has proved much harder to change than was supposed. Looking back with hindsight, the early revisionist writings were too complacent in tone; they proposed the right reforms, but under-rated the difficulty of achieving them in a British context. We were optimists then, though we soon learned our lesson; after the 1959 election defeat I wrote in near-despair that, 'a dogged resistance to change now blankets every segment of our national life.'

Admittedly Conservative administrations have been in power for the greater part of the last two decades. Yet much more should have been achieved by a Labour Government in office and Labour pressure in opposition. Against the dogged resistance to change, we should have pitted a stronger will to change. I conclude that a move to the Left is needed, not in the traditional sense of a move towards old-fashioned Clause 4 Marxism, but in the sense of a sharper delineation of fundamental objectives, a greater clarity about egalitarian priorities and a stronger determination to achieve them.

The rest of this essay discusses what the priorities should be. But a preliminary point must be made. If the Labour Government is to achieve more next time than we did in 1964–70, certain crucial decisions need to be taken and ratified *in advance*; for otherwise our objectives will be lost in the confused hurly-burly and day-to-day crises of government.

Firstly, we must decide that greater equality, and not spawning new pieces of State bureaucracy, is what fundamentally divides us from the Tories.

Secondly, if it is, we must have a concerted strategy for achieving it. This means selecting beforehand a *limited* number of key areas which are to have priority; ensuring that in these areas we have costed, detailed and practical egalitarian policies;

and for the remaining areas demanding a Prime Ministerial directive, that before any decision is taken, whether in the field of taxation or land-use planning or airports policy, the question is always asked and (as far as possible) answered: *cui bono?* Who will be the gainers and who the losers, and what will be the effects on the distribution of welfare?

Thirdly, we must decide to establish a monitoring system to measure the progress in the field of social policy. There are already innumerable *economic* indicators, accounting techniques and annual reports; equivalent *social* indicators are urgently needed and an annual Social Report to test our performance in reducing poverty and inequality. Much work has been done in the U.S.A. in attempting to construct such indicators; and in certain fields there are without doubt huge difficulties. But an essential preliminary, as Professor Robert Neild argued many years ago, would be to establish a central government social unit, parallel to the Treasury economic units, to measure, however crudely at the start, our progress in social policy.

What then are the priority areas in the domestic field? (I assume that a sharp increase in our support for the developing countries is the priority for overseas policy.) They must surely be as follows:

1. To reduce the amount of poverty.
2. To enable everyone to have a decent home.
3. To take development land into public ownership.
4. To redistribute capital wealth.
5. To eliminate selection and segregation in school education.
6. To extend industrial democracy.

The obvious omission is the improvement of the environment, which is temperamentally extremely dear to my heart. I omit it solely because environmental improvement is not a single, separate and isolated objective, but one which must colour our policies in almost every field—housing, regional, transport, industrial and so on. But if I were asked my priority for a short Bill to be passed on the first day of the next Labour

Government, I would choose a savagely penal Bill to curb the odious depredations of commercial property developers.

I shall say nothing more on the housing objective, which is sufficiently discussed in later chapters (though since they were written the country's housing situation has greatly worsened). Nor shall I say more on the public ownership of land (though it will do more to transfer real power and wealth than all the other nationalization proposals put together) or educational reform, since these are areas where the Party has a fully worked-out policy. I concentrate on the three remaining priority areas.

Firstly, the attack on poverty—the overriding moral imperative for a Labour Government. If we treat poverty as being a relative concept, then in some sense we can never eliminate it. But what we can do is both raise the incomes of the poorest 20 per cent *relative* to those of the remaining 80 per cent, and at the same time so markedly increase their *absolute* incomes that any person of compassionate common sense would agree that poverty had diminished. Both these things occurred, for example, to the Negro population of the U.S.A. during the Johnson era as a result of higher social spending combined with economic expansion.

An anti-poverty programme must be based on a combination of more jobs, more services and more income. Full employment and a tight labour market are an absolute prerequisite; for not only is an unemployed man nearly always poorer than one with a job, but those thrown out of work by a recession are likely to be those with other handicaps as well—the older workers and the disabled. Full employment is also the single most effective remedy for low pay.

When I turn to services in kind, I am not speaking of one single anti-poverty social service; but of all the aspects of a modern welfare state ... housing, health care, education, urban transport, youth centres, home helps and the rest. Now the total amount of money spent on these services is enormous; but for two reasons it has been ineffective in diminishing poverty and inequality. Firstly, as I demonstrate later in respect of housing, this has not been given or accepted as an explicit objective; hence the results of social expenditure are often perverse, with the most help going to those least in need. Thus the vastly increased *gross* sums going out in social programmes have produced a disproportionately small improvement in the *net* flow accruing to those in need; so poverty and inequality persist despite a major rise in public expenditure. Secondly, and partly due to this lack of clear objective, there has been too little co-ordination, notably in the inner urban areas of greatest deprivation. The first deficiency will be corrected only if we take and ratify the decisions mentioned above. The second requires that all the 'compensatory' special programmes—urban aid, Educational Priority Areas and so on —should be made the responsibility of a single Minister and a single department in local authorities, and that voluntary community groups should similarly co-ordinate their activities.

To make the poor less poor, we need above all to raise their incomes. At present there is a muddled, piecemeal rag-bag of often means-tested income supplements, which some critics would like to replace by a single basic scheme of guaranteed annual income—a social dividend, income guarantee or negative income-tax. I am not competent to pronounce on such long-term proposals. But it is clear what the immediate priorities are: namely, to increase the non-means-tested benefits going to the elderly, the handicapped and the disabled. The Labour Party now has positive and costed proposals in this field, covering both the benefits and the taxes to finance them. But these must be set in the framework of a *total* anti-poverty programme, covering services in kind as well as cash benefits. We shall no doubt fail to cover everything, for the price of trying to be completely comprehensive is paralysis. But the price of a piecemeal, haphazard approach is that nothing substantial is achieved. We must have at least a limited set of priorities; I am sure that this will not occur unless we establish the machinery and monitoring described above.

Secondly, the redistribution of wealth. I have argued in the past that this will be achieved by: (a) the public ownership of land, for that is where the biggest fortunes are both made and inherited; (b) the taxation of capital gains as income (and not at a lower rate as now); (c) a wealth tax; (d) a tax on gifts, integrated with death duties and embodying the principle of progression according to size of bequest. These proposals still seem valid; though the last three could probably be simplified and refined into an annual graduated wealth tax and a single progressive tax on the receipt of all gifts and legacies.

An important new proposal has recently been added to this list.[28] Stimulated by Danish initiatives, both Professor Atkinson and a Labour Party Study Group have suggested a capital growth-sharing scheme which would in effect be a tax on existing shareholders. Companies would transfer annually (say) 1 per cent of their outstanding equity (or the equivalent in cash) to a National Workers' Fund, in which all workers in all industries would participate equally through a growing annual entitlement. This would redistribute wealth from shareholders to workers, and give the labour force a genuine and growing stake in the expansion of the economy.

There is still some confusion in the minds of the authors as to how far the Fund is to use its shareholdings to exercise control (e.g. in pushing firms into more 'social' and less profitable behaviour) and how far to maximize the capital wealth of the workers; it is not always understood that these two functions are not only in conflict, but also require quite different types of expertise. But this Fund, alongside a growing National Superannuation Fund, would provide the appropriate means whereby the community could steadily increase its stake and share-holding in British industry.

It should be understood by now that higher capital taxation of the rich will not solve all the public expenditure problems; it helps only to the extent that it reduces the *consumption* of the rich; and the amounts involved here are comparatively small in relation to G.N.P. The object is different. The institution of inheritance, the natural forces of accumulation, the biological transmission of skills and the grim law of 'to him that hath, shall be given' would, if left unchecked, lead to a cumulative increase in inequality. Against this tendency we must pit the forces of social democracy. Offensive inequalities still remain and must be reduced, less today on the classic redistributional welfare grounds, than in order to create a more just society; especially in Britain, scarred as we are by unusually deep class divisions in other, non-monetary spheres.

Thirdly, industrial democracy. Ten years ago scarcely a whisper was heard on this subject at Labour or trade union conferences; today there is a dramatic upsurge of interest. This is not due to any decline in the bargaining power of the workers or their unions; on the contrary, that power has continued to grow in conditions of full employment and inflation. But it has grown less fast than the demands and aspirations of the working (and salaried) classes.

Despite increased prosperity, there is a growing revolt against authoritarian management, the boredom of dull and monotonous jobs, the exigencies of the production-line, the smell and dirt and noise of factory life. Indeed the greater prosperity increases the resentment, for it sharpens the contrast between work conditions and leisure conditions; the factory worker with a decent home and a car, able to travel at weekends and on holiday, is less willing to tolerate uncivilized conditions at work. So there is a greater amount of industrial unrest, absenteeism and rapid labour turnover, and a strong, though inchoate, demand for a more direct control over working conditions.

The growth in industrial unrest has two even more elemental causes: the fear of inflation (already discussed) and the fear of losing a job. With technological change so rapid and competition so acute, workers are constantly anxious that the bottom may drop out of the market for the goods which they are producing. The fear of lay-offs and redundancies is deep and pervasive in all ranks of the working class; the more so since the level of aspirations and the pattern of consumption (with

D

its hire-purchase and, increasingly, even mortgage commitments) now make a break in income-flow exceptionally painful. It is these facts, even more than the much-publicized revolt
against mass-production, which explain the extent of current
unrest.[29]

The desire for more industrial democracy must be supported
by socialists not only for humanitarian reasons, but also on
grounds of equality; for there are wide disparities between
middle-class and working-class occupations in respect both of
conditions of work and job security. How can it be achieved in
practice?

There is no dispute in Britain about what should be done at
the crucial shop-floor level, which is where it matters most.
Here trade union collective bargaining has already enforced a
measure of workers' control through the joint regulation of
wages, conditions of work, overtime, discipline, manning and
promotion. This collective bargaining should be formalized
still further at the level of the plant, and extended both to
occupations where it scarcely yet exists, and also to cover the
structure, organization and environment of work as well as the
traditional 'wage' questions. Since so much of the present discontent and inequality is rooted in *local* and shop-floor conditions, the extension of local bargaining is a key element in
industrial democracy.

But no amount of local *plant* bargaining will give the workers control over *company* management decisions—on location
of investment, closures or mergers; the question here is the
balance of power in the government of the firm, and how to
alter that balance in favour of the workers.

The best way of doing so is again to extend the principle of
collective bargaining—from plant bargaining over wages and
work to bargaining at company level over the whole range of
managerial functions, including the formulation and application
of the company's corporate plan. For today no area of company
decision-taking is beyond the rightful concern of the work-
force; sole managerial prerogative is a thing of the past; any

subject is a proper one for the negotiating table. High-level 'predictive bargaining' (as McCarthy and Ellis call it)[30] will not banish industrial conflict or differences of interest; and third-party techniques for resolving disputes will be even more necessary than now. But it may be the most meaningful way of extending industrial democracy.

It will, however, be a long and complex task; and more and more people want to take a short cut and put worker-representatives directly on the boards of companies. I have, in the past, been sceptical about this, believing that the strength of the unions depended on their remaining independent of management and exercising an opposition role; and this has been the traditional view of the British unions. But their failure to influence or prevent the spate of closures, rationalizations and redundancies in recent years has caused them to re-think their position. Moreover the German Left, after two decades of experience, has become markedly more enthusiastic about co-determination; and the Scandinavian countries are moving in the same direction. The talk is now everywhere of two-tier management with worker representatives on the top-tier Supervisory Board.

I strongly sympathize with the desire of the unions to be represented at the heart of the decision-making process, though whether this calls for a division of the whole of the management function into 'supervision' and 'executive management' on the Continental model is another question. But two problems are left unanswered by the T.U.C.'s recent statement which (going beyond the Scandinavian proposals) calls for 50 per cent union representation on the Supervisory Board.[31] The first is how decisions are to be reached when the two sides on a Board are deadlocked. The second is how the unions are to preserve credibility with their membership when, through their representatives on the Supervisory Board, they are forced to associate themselves with decisions which run counter to the immediate interests of their rank-and-file.

The answer seems to lie in the appointment, on the German

model, of an independent 'eleventh man' to the Supervisory
Board. It would be his role to arbitrate between the two sides
in cases of disagreement; and his existence would permit the
Union representatives to disassociate themselves from particular Board decisions, and tell the management that this time they
must go it alone, without simultaneously causing the whole
enterprise to grind to a halt. The trade unions would thus be
full partners in a coalition, but without totally sacrificing their
adversary role and ultimate rights of opposition.

One must not expect revolutionary changes from union
participation in management (and opinion surveys show that it
does not come high on the list of working-class priorities).
The worker-directors may become as remote from their
rank-and-file as some local councillors or members of regional
hospital boards are now. They may find themselves becoming
dangerously compromised and equivocal in their loyalties.
The system may break down because it is not co-ordinated with
other Labour proposals; for example, the Executive Board of a
firm may find its price and investment decisions first altered by
the Supervisory Board, then modified as a result of a Planning
Agreement, next vetoed by the National Workers' Fund, then
reinstated by the National Enterprise Board and finally
rejected by the Price Commission—why, oh why, can we
never co-ordinate our various policies? And finally one must
remember that the interests of the workers in a plant are not
always the same as those of consumers or the whole community. Workers' control is not the same as social control; the
Labour Party is not a syndicalist party.

So one must see participation in management as one element,
and not the most important, in a total programme for industrial
democracy and greater equality of working conditions: a
programme to be achieved partly by legislation and partly by
trade union pressure, and covering the whole spectrum of work
organization—job security, personnel policies, the planning
of factories, the proportion of the old and disabled to be employed, health and safety, pollution by noise and dirt and fumes,

and (where possible) the reorganization of production, to restore to the individual worker the responsibility for controlling the way he does his job. For the 'alienation' of the worker cannot be ascribed, as it was by Marx, to the system of property relations; it is rooted in the technological processes of large-scale industrialization and the job insecurity bred by rapid change. It is in these respects that workers want more say in the decision-making process; and industrial democracy is one way of achieving this.

Here is a programme of reform which should challenge and stimulate all democratic socialists. Yet the present mood seems to be one, not of hopeful and purposive optimism as it was twenty years ago, but of pessimism, lack of clarity, a flight into chiliasm and a loss of practical radical will-power.

The intelligentsia, always prone to the liberal rhetoric of catastrophe, has adopted an apocalyptic mood, denying (against the facts) that reformist progress can be made and believing in any case that ecological disaster is just over the horizon. Industrial militancy is on the increase, but often with competitive and sectional rather than socialist goals in mind. The stability of democratic society and the possibility of peaceful reform seem more and more threatened by angry workers, students, squatters and even middle-class amenity groups. Children invade the sacred pitch at Lords; Tory conferences echo to the unprecedented sound of hissing and booing; every planning decision now goes to appeal. Even the rule of law is challenged by some Labour councillors and trade unionists, though historically—and let no socialist ever forget this—the law has been the means by which the weak obtained redress against the strong.

I believe a new mood to exist, though I think it to be much exaggerated by the press and the media. 'Too large a generalization', wrote Alfred North Whitehead, 'leads to mere barrenness'; and we are suffering from a surfeit of large generalizations. For example, attitude surveys which seek to probe the depth of dissatisfaction with jobs or living standards, consistently fail to reveal a mass revolt against the whole system. Manifestations of discontent—group violence, civil disturbance, racial strife, political extremism, student unrest, drug-taking, the underground press—wax and wane with bewildering unpredictability. At the present time they seem greatly on the wane as compared with five years ago.[32] How they will seem five years hence—or even next year—I have no idea; for there are no means of accurately predicting the diastole and systole of our restless and uncertain society.

That there is *some* increase in discontent, one can have little doubt. It has nothing to do with the ownership of the means of production, though labour leaders sometimes rationalize it in these terms; nor is it in any accepted sense a move to the Left—indeed it takes a non-ideological (if not positively anti-ideological) form. There is largely a growing (and welcome) assertion of democratic rights, and a refusal automatically to accept the *fiat* of management, bureaucracies and men and women in authority. There are specific economic discontents to which I have alluded earlier. The British people have seen both major parties trying to grapple with the economic problems, and not succeeding. Above all inflation, creating as it does a menacing insecurity about the future and threatening to erase all our familiar bench-marks, induces a mood of anxious yet militant resentment.

But this mood of discontent, though often (and naturally enough, given the fact of inflation) selfish and negative rather than radical and positive, makes it more essential, not less, to strive for a more just and equal society. Of course there are constraints on what can be done to alter society in a five-year term of office. Each of the six areas described above throws up complex problems of internal priorities which have certainly not all been resolved in current Labour thinking. Each will impose heavy and conflicting demands on Parliamentary time, Ministerial capacity, and the Whitehall machine (however much enlarged or reformed). And results take time to achieve; one cannot train a single doctor or build a single hospital (or even an aluminium smelter) within the lifetime of a Parliament.

It is therefore vital not to create excessive expectations. The public is often cynical about politicians, yet paradoxically expects too much of the political system. Politicians, caught up in the, now almost permanent, atmosphere of rabid electioneering, themselves encourage the question: 'What have you done for us lately?' An increasingly educated public, with higher aspirations in all directions, makes more and more incompatible demands; government is asked to perform marvels, though the achievement of one marvel often rules out the possibility of another. Marx was constantly nervous lest the revolution should occur before he had completed the text of *Das Kapital*. But democratic systems are slow to alter; it takes some time to produce a fundamental and irreversible transfer of power and wealth.

The biggest constraint in many areas is of course public expenditure. This, on account of demographic trends, rising standards, increasing costs and new demands (e.g. in the environmental sphere) is the central problem facing all developed societies. It is especially acute, as the Scandinavian socialist parties have been compelled to realize, for a left-wing party whose specifically *socialist* aims call for a yet further degree of communal spending.

Socialists must be unapologetic about this, and about its implications for taxation. But we must also be honest with our supporters. The extra money cannot all be painlessly found out of the consumption of the rich (though that will be reduced by the measures described earlier) or the share of profit in G.N.P. (which is certainly not too high given the continuing need for more investment) or by taking up slack in the economy (for if there is any slack in the economy which we inherit, it will surely be pre-empted to correct a balance of payments deficit). We shall require higher taxation of the whole better-off section of the community, which now includes some trade unionists (for example, in the docks, engineering, printing) who believe more strongly in differentials than in equality.

But if the growth-rate is low, higher taxation leaves little or nothing for increased consumer expenditure; and, as I showed in an earlier section, a severe squeeze on personal incomes and spending provokes (though it is not the only cause of) a violent inflation.

Inflation is becoming more and more our central problem—the problem which, along with lagging productivity, sometimes makes the British economy seem unmanageable. It has no single cause and no single remedy. The only countries with virtually no (open) inflation are the Communist countries (with the exception of the relatively liberal Yugoslavia); and they (like Nazi Germany before them) have achieved this by monolithic state control and the suppression of free trade unions. In democratic countries some inflation is clearly endemic, being rooted in our free institutions, political structure and insistent determination always to demand more than our total resources can supply. It is, moreover, aggravated in modern societies by the continuous growth in service employment; for while in the manufacturing sector, where productivity gains are high, wage increases can be absorbed without an excessive rise in prices, this is not true of the growing service sector to which these wage increases are communicated. One cannot achieve equivalent productivity gains in medical care, schooling, recreation or insurance; so there are not only higher prices for canteen meals and holidays and car insurance, but also (since so many services are publicly provided) higher taxes and local rates.

Whatever the rate of growth, inflation is an issue of overriding importance which should be the subject of the most frank and detailed joint talks between the Labour Party and the unions—talks in which the Party asks the unions to make more concessions as well as making concessions itself. For it is the purest wishful thinking to suppose that in an increasingly planned economy (especially when a growing part of the population is employed in the public sector) governments can adopt a *dirigiste* attitude to the control of prices, but a laissez-faire attitude to the determination of incomes; the more so since this would involve abandoning one possible means of achieving a greater equality of incomes.

But for a Labour Government wishing to re-allocate resources on a considerable scale, slow growth is an additional cause of inflation. We must, in order to finance our collective spending, reduce the *share* of consumption in total income. But this (for reasons which I discussed earlier) can only be done without extra inflation if the *absolute* level of consumption is rising steadily; and that requires a rapid rate of growth.

The objective of faster growth has recently come under attack on ecological and environmental grounds. I argue in later chapters that we should strongly resist this attack. Faster growth is wholly consistent with a better environment, less pollution and a slower increase in population; and without it we shall find it infinitely harder to eliminate poverty, reduce inequality and generally allocate our wealth in the manner which we as socialists desire. The environmental argument, and the possible shortage of (for example) energy supplies, strengthen the case for social control and intervention in markets. How we allocate our growing wealth within, and still more between, nations becomes an ever more central question. But then that is what socialism was always about.

By more rapid growth, I do not mean an insensate pursuit of growth (not that I can conceive of such a thing in the British climate of opinion) or one neglectful of the environment. I mean planned and controlled growth up to the limit of our productive potential—say, 4 per cent per annum. While this would still be below the rate achieved in most other advanced countries, it would be nearly double the 2·3 per cent rate of 1964–70 (and my heart freezes when I think of what we could have achieved in those years with double the additional resources). I discuss in a later essay the pre-conditions of growing at this rate; and Mr Michael Stewart analyses them more fully in an admirable Fabian publication.[33]

But we do not know whether we can achieve them; for we do not have some panacea for crisis-free growth which was mysteriously hidden from both the previous Labour and the present Tory Governments. Moreover, the higher cost of oil, even after the temporary disruption is over, may slow down growth in the entire industrialized world (though in the medium term Britain is exceptionally well-placed for energy supplies). And whatever the rate of growth we have to remember that our socialist claims on the increment are not always the same as those of the mass of our supporters. While we rightly say that equality and higher public expenditure are what divide us from the Tories, they may reply that their priorities are more jobs, lower prices, lower taxes or the suppression of crime.

Here is the basic dilemma facing all democratic socialist parties; for we owe strong moral obligations to the ordinary people who support us. The dilemma will be more easily resolved if we have a faster rate of growth. But whatever the rate of growth, we can, and must, mount a determined attack on specific social evils and specific inequalities. And so we must ruthlessly select priorities. We must prepare in advance a limited programme of radical measures which do not promise more than we can actually perform, which are closely related to the needs and aspirations of ordinary people, and yet which constitute a coherent egalitarian strategy instead of a muddle of bits and pieces. Diffusion of effort is the enemy of social progress. Only if we concentrate our effort shall we make a significant advance towards greater justice and equality.

2 Socialists in a Dangerous World

The text of an address given at a Socialist Commentary meeting during the Labour Party Conference at Blackpool in October 1968, at a time when the fortunes of the Labour Government appeared at their lowest. The talk was reprinted as a supplement to Socialist Commentary *in November 1968.*

I start by asking what went wrong. What correct diagnosis of the long and dramatic descent from the triumph of the 1966 General Election to the disasters of 1968 can be made? I think it probable, though none of us can prove it, that the obvious diagnosis is the correct one.

We inherited an economy that had for some time been sluggish by international standards and in 1964 was in the throes of an acute balance of payments crisis. We took at the start the basic decision not to alter the exchange rate. Instead, we had recourse to a purely temporary import control in the form of the import surcharge, followed by a marked degree of deflation in July 1966, all combined with what turns out, looking back, to have been an over-optimistic belief that long-term measures of planning and intervention (such as incomes policy, the National Plan, restructuring of industry, and so on) would achieve rapid results.

This mixture failed and in consequence we had three years of a rate of economic growth of only 1–1½ per cent per annum—the longest period of slow growth since 1945. And although in this period the standard of living has been cushioned by massive borrowing from overseas, the result nevertheless was a sharp increase in unemployment in the regions, last winter's unpopular cuts in public expenditure, the myth, if not the reality, that

real wages were under harsh attack, and, above all, a general
sense of continuing crisis and failure.

Now of course there are other possible explanations of our
loss of popularity. Some of these, I confess, evoke in me only
incredulity, such as the notion that the Labour Government
has moved to the right of its traditional supporters, where I find
all the evidence, alas, to be the other way around. Others are
couched in more grandiose terms of 'a wholesale alienation
from the system', or a 'a total breakdown of communications',
or 'a revolutionary realignment of political loyalties' or a
malaise analogous with that of the pre-1914 period. These
theories, like so many others that have their origin in SW1 or
EC4, I find difficult to translate into the realities of my Grimsby
constituency. I therefore assume, especially as the simple diagnosis is in itself a plausible and sufficient one, that it is probably
the correct one.

I now turn to prognosis. Fortunately the atmosphere today
is markedly different from what it was six months ago. Then,
for the first time that I can remember, I found myself seriously
at odds with many old friends and allies in past struggles. They
were arguing, it appeared to me, that the next election was
already lost; it could be taken as written off, and there was little
that we could do about it. There was a general atmosphere, particularly perhaps amongst intellectuals, of defeatism and despair.
Now I thought then, and still think, that this attitude showed a
certain loss of nerve and failure of will, but above all, a complete lack of historical sense; for surely both history and contemporary experience teach us that the only certain thing about
democratic politics is its uncertainty.

One could, of course, find endless examples of this from
history, but I choose one or two examples from the post-war
period. Who amongst us predicted in 1957 the result of the
1959 election, or at the time of the disastrous Leyton by-election, in January 1965, the result of the 1966 election? How many
in the United States in 1947 prophesied the Truman victory of
1948? Or a year ago foresaw the shape and character of the

current Presidential election? Who in this hall foresaw last year the events of this spring in France, or the landslide victory of the Swedish Social Democrats a month ago?

So when I take, as I do and did even at our lowest period at the beginning of this year, the robust and confident view that we can perfectly well win the next election, I have the full support of logic and historical experience.

But how do we do it? I must start off with the obvious judgment that full economic recovery is a necessary condition of victory, and indeed the foundation on which our whole strategy must rest. This is so partly because the personal standard of living must have some influence on voting attitudes (although precisely how much I shall discuss in a moment), partly because economic growth is essential to carrying out our general social objectives, and above all, because economic success is crucial to the standing of any government and the confidence felt in it by the voters: particularly perhaps for a Labour Government which is always in danger of being thought less competent, less businesslike and more prone to muddle than a Conservative Government.

So I have no doubts that success in our economic strategy is a vitally necessary condition for victory. But the question is: is it also a sufficient condition, even if it culminates, as many hope, in a final phase of popular Budgets and rising personal consumption? I think that it is not. The short-term interaction between the standard of living and voting attitudes is extremely unpredictable, and sometimes even perverse. For example, last winter an exceptionally large boom in consumer spending coincided with Labour's sinking to its lowest point of electoral unpopularity. 1967 as a whole was a year in which real wages rose while the Government's popularity steadily fell. This I think, may well reflect a longer-term change: the fact that after more than two decades of post-war experience, full employment and rising living standards are increasingly taken for granted, and do not swing votes between one party and another on the same scale as in the past.

More recently, for example in the current American election, the Democrats are in danger of being deserted precisely by the prosperous and fully employed white workers for whom they have done most. Taking movements like Scottish Nationalism, or recent events in France, one finds large swings of opinion which cannot be linked in any simple way with changes in material prosperity. In the recent Swedish election, indeed, a rise in unemployment has the perverse effect of markedly helping the existing Social-Democratic Government.

In any case, if we were to ask to be judged by the sole criterion of material prosperity, apart from whether any of us would then want to continue actively in politics, surely people would say, 'Well, if that is all there is to it, if this is simply a question of individual material success, then let us have the Tories. They will do it better because it is more in line with their philosophy.' So I conclude that the famous jingle of the half-crown in the pocket, although of course it is one relevant factor, is not a 100 per cent guarantee of electoral success.

What else, then, do we need? I do not believe that we need some fundamental rethinking of socialism, or a mass of new policies. Indeed, I think the constant call for new policies or dramatic new statements is a sign of a rather hysterical reaction to temporary electoral unpopularity. The situation is not at all the same as it was in the 1950s when *Socialist Commentary*, like myself, was concerned with a basic re-analysis of Labour philosophy. We then faced a situation fundamentally different from that of the 1930s, when the traditional Labour policy had been formulated.

That is not the position today. The essential social problems of 1964 are still the same in 1968; and despite a considerable achievement in the last four years—a good deal larger, incidentally, than many critics are prepared to allow—many of them still cry out urgently for solution. Of course there are also new issues, which require new policies or new attitudes; I shall touch on some of these later. But what is most needed today is not some great shift of policy but a reaffirmation of our agreed social-democratic ideals, which are still totally relevant to our situation in Britain and still very far from being realized.

I do not want today to catalogue these ideals, on which I have written much, and which would be both familiar to, and agreed by, almost everybody in this hall. Rather, I want to discuss some more general issues which are crucial to the attainment of our objectives.

My first point is the issue of public expenditure, since many of the desired reforms will require a substantial increase in public spending. How is this to be achieved? Once again, the first and essential condition is economic growth; without that, there is no hope of the increase we want. But in addition I believe that we need to re-examine thoroughly the tax system which, as compared with that in some other industrial countries, yields a lower proportion of the national income in revenue, yet with a louder outcry of popular complaint. We need to make an equally thorough re-examination of the content and definitions of public expenditure, so that we do not gratuitously alarm the International Monetary Fund and foreign bankers by treating it all as one single lump sum, in which productive investment in aluminium smelters or shipyards is equated with 'wicked' expenditure on old age pensions.

But, much more difficult than any of this, we shall need to conduct a sustained and continuous attack on certain popular attitudes, which on such issues as race, civil liberties or foreign affairs, are often reactionary. Here we face a crucial moral choice: whether to accept these attitudes and defer to them, or to seek to alter them by the exercise of leadership. Now we shall certainly not be able to exercise this leadership if we give way to a mood which I sensed was growing in the party some months ago: a certain mood of cynicism, a certain loss of radical will-power, a feeling (perhaps a natural, but still an undesirable, response to electoral unpopularity) that everything had to be subordinated to the supposed instant reactions of public opinion. This mood has been evident, to take some examples, in much recent discussion of the public schools issue, of family allowances and of foreign aid. The tendency is to say, 'It's too difficult, too costly, too unpopular to do what we think to be right.'

Naturally we must keep a balance. Nobody wants to ignore public opinion. We all want to win the next election; we are not in politics for the pleasure of useless protest. Nevertheless I think the pendulum has swung too far the other way. For reasons I gave earlier, I do not think election victories can be guaranteed by concentrating solely on people's private standard of living. I therefore believe that we need to take some risks, to exert a positive leadership, to catch a glimpse of some kind of vision other than a rise in personal spending, and to create again a sense of valid idealism so that we can offer the electorate, when we come to face them, a positive and distinctive policy.

My second general point concerns the fact, which will become increasingly relevant to many of our decisions, of a growing divergence in our highly technological society between private and social benefit. I refer to those numerous cases where a certain course of action is advantageous to manufacturers, to operators or to some private citizens, but imposes major costs on the rest of the community, typically in the form of loss of comfort or amenity, for example, aircraft noise, diesel fumes or the steady pollution of the sea and rivers. I mention here one interesting test-case, which is the Stansted issue. I hope that the Roskill Commission will not only recommend a site for the third London Airport, but will analyse generally the question of what sort of monetary price one should be willing to pay in the country in order to preserve amenity and avoid some of the adverse consequences of modern technology.

In that particular case it may be mainly a matter of money. But in other cases it may be a matter of restricting the rights of private individuals in the interests of the common good. Where this is a choice that we have to make, I hope that we shall learn the lesson of the breathalyzer and realize that such decisions, while they may incur temporary unpopularity, will in the end, prove not merely beneficial but also fully acceptable to public opinion.

My third point concerns the burning question of how we cope in Britain with a likely rise in population of fifteen to twenty million by the end of the century. There are many aspects to this problem: the total pressure on resources, the balance between the regions, the preservation of the country-side and so on. But what concerns me most is how we plan the urban centres of the future. Much of the post-war urban planning has been aesthetically horrible. But, more important, so many of the post-war housing estates seem not to have provided the three things that I think most people want from their environment—a proper degree of privacy, a sense of space and amenity and some feeling of community. I think this whole problem of accommodating a large increase in population in a small island, while maintaining or creating a civilized environment, must come increasingly to dominate our thinking.

This leads me naturally to my next point, and that is the question of participation—currently the favourite word in SW1 or EC4. I think this is a most important concept, particularly as we seem to have a rather weak sense of community in Britain at the present time, but I find myself out of sympathy with much of the current discussion for it appears to me to imply certain things which are either impossible, or undesirable or irrelevant to the end in view.

I say impossible, because if what is meant by participation is an active and continuous process of participating in decision-making, then all experience shows that only a small minority of the population will wish to participate. This seems to be so whether one takes attendance at trade union branch meetings, or whether one takes more recent examples (with many of which I have been closely associated) such as the Consumer Association, or CASE or local civic societies, all of which remain after many years of hard endeavour essentially minority and largely middle-class groups. Now I would certainly like (within limits which I mention in a moment) to see significantly more

E

such participation, and would expect to see it with the spread of education. But the fact is that the majority will continue to prefer to lead a full family life and cultivate their gardens.

And a very good thing too. For a continuous political activism by the great bulk of the population would not only run counter to most people's desires for privacy and a leisured family life, but it would also (as G. D. H. Cole used often to say) pose a real threat to the stability of our democracy. Indeed it would mark the breakdown of normal social cohesion.

I also, as I said, find much of the current discussion irrelevant to the end in view. For whatever is the true case for participation (I shall come to that in a minute), it has little to do with the kind of constitutional changes which are often urged when the subject is under discussion, and which frequently amount to representation on some remote body. For example, worker-directors on the board of I.C.I., or elected regional councils or new high-level national tripartite bodies, may all be highly desirable, but they will not much increase the sense of participation in Grimsby. True, there are certain constitutional changes and acts of devolution that are needed to make British democracy more effective. We need to make considerable changes in parliamentary procedure in order that the executive can be more sensitive to the legislature than it is at present. Much more vital, we must quickly decide on how we react, if we should react, to the tide of nationalism in Scotland and Wales; from a party-political point of view this is the most urgent decision facing us at this moment.

But high-level constitutional changes do not meet the real problem raised by this discussion. What most people want, in my view, is neither high-level constitutional change nor a continuous process of active participation. They want the right to be consulted about, and to influence, particular decisions which affect their daily lives; they want an effective machinery for the redress of grievances; and they want proper power to enforce that right and that machinery.

But this kind of participation has its reality at a local and not a national level. For example, in industry, this is not mainly a matter of high-level representation on national boards, desirable as that may be, but of the active power of trade unions and shop stewards at plant level: that I have always thought was the true meaning of industrial democracy. (I suppose, as judged by this, the motor industry recently has shown the highest degree of industrial democracy the world has ever seen.) In higher education, it is not a matter of giving representation to the National Union of Students on the University Grants Committee, desirable as that may or may not be, but of particular arrangements in particular colleges and universities. And in local government, where the need is greater than anywhere else, it is not a matter of new forms of local or regional government, again, desirable or not as they may be, but of effective power to influence decisions concerning particular schools, particular hospitals, particular housing estates and, perhaps most of all, particular planning policies.

This, to my mind, is where the next step forward ought to come. It will need not only a less passive and indifferent attitude on the part of a number of our citizens; it will also need the strengthening of existing, and the creation of new, local pressure-groups and institutions, since democratic reform can ultimately only come through institutions.

The central role of institutions leads me to the last point which I want to discuss, and that is one aspect of the current student revolt. Now I do not think that anyone can accurately diagnose either the cause, the scope or the significance of this revolt. One cannot tell whether it will prove a continuing phenomenon, or be as ephemeral as (say) the post-1918 revolutionary communist movement in the West which, after brief triumphs in Hungary and Bavaria, was effectively over by 1920. Nor indeed, despite the brilliant articles by *Insight* journalists bringing them all together, can one ascribe the events in different countries to a single cause or pattern; they cannot all be explained, for example, by the Vietnam war, any more than youthful unrest a decade ago (if only because it coincided with a sharp rise in the birthrate everywhere) could be explained by deep anxiety about the nuclear bomb. Nor, lastly, can one attach the same degree of moral significance to all these events—to the current demonstrations in the Philippines, to student bravery in Prague, to the occurrences at the Frankfurt Book Fair or to the struggle of the Spanish students.

But in so far as one can try to make distinctions, I suppose that one has mixed feelings. One feels sympathy towards the general irreverence and disrespect for established authority and entrenched ideas. One must sympathize with the revolt against archaic, obsolete and paternalistic systems of higher education, whether in British art colleges or French universities; certainly we have no right to complain so long as we fail to satisfy legitimate grievances here. And above all, on a wholly different plane of moral seriousness, one feels total sympathy in those cases where student revolt is an aspect, if not, indeed, the spearhead, of a popular revolt against foreign or domestic tyranny, whether in Czechoslovakia or in Spain.

On the other hand one feels unsympathetic if student revolt, under the guise of fighting oppression, becomes itself intolerant and authoritarian, as when its theorists bitterly attack 'the consumer society' regardless of whether or not this is what most people want.

In particular, one feels totally unsympathetic (or one should), when in democratic countries the revolt manifests itself in deliberate violence of a traditional extremist kind, even though under new political labels. Such violence inevitably calls forth against itself a more powerful counter-reaction and counter-violence, as in France recently or today in the United States. A refusal to compromise will always lead to authoritarianism, whether in the family, in industry, in social groups or in a nation. Violence is never justified unless it is the sole method of establishing democracy; otherwise it becomes itself a weapon against democracy, reflecting a derision for the rights of the majority and a contempt for the right of free speech. (In this connection it is well to remember that the extremist students are not merely a minority of all *students*; they wholly fail to reflect, to judge by recent opinion surveys, the political attitudes of young people as a whole.) I confess I find something faintly nauseating about the 'drawing-room' or vicarious flirtation with violence, which sometimes emanates from Great Turnstile or the Orkneys and Shetlands. It reminds me of a poignant passage in *Dr Zhivago*, where Pasternak writes that, 'men like Pamphil, who needed no encouragement to hate intellectuals, officers and gentry with a savage hatred, were regarded by enthusiastic left-wing intellectuals as a rare find and were greatly valued. Their inhumanity seemed a marvel of class consciousness, their barbarism a model of proletarian firmness and revolutionary instinct.'

But the particular point that I want to make concerns one aspect of the philosophy, not of course of the majority of students, but of the radical element of the New Left; that is, the belief that in the pursuit of 'participatory democracy' the State and all other institutions should be destroyed. Now the fact is, and we must face this as rational social-democrats, that there is no substitute for institutions, with their bureaucracy, rules, clerks and computers. Of course one must reform or replace them if they become ossified, but one cannot simply abolish them; they are the only instruments of social reform. This is an obvious and basic truth.

But it is especially true today when there are three overwhelming threats on which political discussion must increasingly fasten, and any of which could bring civilization to an end. They are the appalling population explosion, as to whose consequences (even more in terms of congestion and overcrowding than of food supply) I am deeply pessimistic; the likelihood of the spread of nuclear weapons to countries which cannot be relied on to control their use; and, perhaps longer term, but increasingly disturbing, the pollution of the environment. Now these three threats, as Nathan Glazer has recently remarked in the American magazine *Commentary*, have one thing in common. If they are to be met and surmounted, they will all call for an increasing degree of social and institutional control. There never, in fact, has been a moment in history when anarchism or utopianism were more dangerous and less appropriate, or when there was a greater need for rigorous analysis combined with a practical determination to change the course of events.

I have not had for a long time a greater sense of the need for our social-democratic traditions of conscience and reform, of radical dissent, of systematic social analysis. At a moment when there is in Britain a real danger of a radical Right extremism, when economic misfortune and loss of momentum threaten our progress towards the reforms we want, when Russian communism has shown itself in its most brutal colours in Czechoslovakia and when the most urgent problems of controlling the environment loom up on the world horizon — at such a moment we all of us need, without hesitation, to reaffirm our faith in social-democratic values.

3 A Social-Democratic Britain

Originally published, under the same title, as a Fabian pamphlet (Tract 404) in January 1971. It is based on a lecture given before a Fabian audience in November 1970, in the aftermath of Labour's electoral defeat in June 1970.

Introduction

After an unexpected election defeat, a party tends for a time to lose its sense of direction; and many people are now asking what Labour really stands for in the 1970s. The answer appears to me glaringly obvious. I am speaking not in terms of detail, but of broad objectives. And the objectives seem to me basically those which most Fabians have believed in for the past ten years or more.

Firstly, an exceptionally high priority, when considering the claims on our resources, for the relief of poverty, distress and social squalor—Labour's traditional 'social welfare' goal.

Secondly, a more equal distribution of wealth, not because redistribution today will make all the workers rich, but to help create a more just and humane society.

Thirdly, a wider ideal of social equality, involving not only educational reform but generally an improvement in our social capital; such that the less well-off have access to housing, health and education of a standard comparable, at least in the basic decencies, to that which the better-off can buy for themselves out of their private means.

Fourthly, strict social control over the environment—to enable us to cope with the exploding problems of urban life, to protect the countryside from the threat posed by more industry, more people and more cars and to diminish the growing divergence between private and social cost in such areas as noise, fumes, river pollution and the rest. (This is also an aspect of social equality, since the rich can often *buy* privacy and protection from these intrusions; only social action can give the less well-off the same protection).

This is not necessarily an exhaustive list; and I discuss later whether there are new objectives of great significance which should be added to it. But when I search my mind, these four aims seem to me to constitute the essence of social democracy in the 1970s. Yet can this really be so? Has so little changed in the last decade that our objectives, however modified, remain basically the same? Should we not rather argue trendily for some fashionable version of the 'new politics'? My answer is firmly 'No.' These four objectives relate to what are still our most urgent social problems; and no one could possibly say that they are within sight of attainment. Even after six years of Labour Government, there is still a stubborn residue of degrading poverty; there are large inequalities of wealth; there are glaring gaps in the provision of housing, health and education; there is a growing environmental problem; in particular, the complex of urban problems, housing, poverty, renewal, traffic, is not within sight of solution; and there are certain problems, such as nursery schools, where a start has barely been made on what needs to be done.

Without doubt, Labour achieved a great deal in many directions—in education, social security, tax reform, regional policy, conservation and environmental planning. But due partly to slow growth and partly to hostile public attitudes, we achieved less than we had hoped and certainly not enough to render our objectives obsolete. There is no analogy with the 1950s, when society had been changed out of recognition since the 1930s by full employment and the Welfare State, and where a fundamental rethinking was required. That is not the position today, and the evidence is the lack of any furious ideological ferment within the Party. Of course we must continuously adapt our detailed policies, and of course new problems will call for new policies, but the basic objectives remain wholly relevant and contemporary. What we need is not some great shift of direction, but a clear reaffirmation of these agreed ideals. These ideals all fundamentally relate to how we distribute wealth and allocate our resources; that is what socialism is about, and what divides the Left from the Right. We shall not get the allocation we want without a certain view of taxation and public expenditure, and of social control and collective responsibility. And we shall not get that without a healthy rate of economic growth.

I start with the question of growth, and a confession of personal error. Looking back, I was too complacent about growth in *The Future of Socialism* (though I had learned my error by the time I wrote *The Conservative Enemy*). I accepted the then official projections, which forecast a nearly stationary population; hence, like others at the time, I did not foresee the huge demands on our resources for housing, education and health, which a rising population brings in its train. And I did not anticipate that successive governments would be so eccentric as to use periodic bouts of deflation, that is, deliberate *reductions* in growth, as almost their only means of regulating the economy.

In the event, the record of economic growth has been lamentable; the facts are dreary and familiar. Over the years the growth-rate has been only half that of most other advanced industrial countries. Britain has been successively overtaken in average living-standards by Sweden, Australia, Canada, Germany, France, Switzerland, New Zealand, Denmark, Norway, Holland and Belgium. By 1980, on present trends, she will have been overtaken by Japan (spectacularly) and Finland, and possibly by Austria and Italy. And the performance is not improving. The annual growth-rate over the last five years of 2·2 per cent was lower than in the previous decade (an almost sufficient explanation of Labour's defeat last June) and it is not certain that the growth-rate will even reach 2 per cent in 1970.

This wretched showing, for which all of us who were in Government must share responsibility, exacts a calamitous cost in terms of welfare (both public and private). Certainly we cannot even approach our basic objectives with the present rate of growth. For these objectives, as I have said, require a redistribution of wealth and resources; and we shall not get this unless the *total* resources are growing rapidly.

I do not of course mean that rapid growth will automatically produce a transfer of resources of the kind we want; whether it does or not will depend on the social and political values of the country concerned. But I do assert dogmatically that in a democracy low or zero growth wholly excludes the possibility. For any substantial transfer then involves not merely a relative but an *absolute* decline in the real incomes of the better-off half of the population (which incidentally includes large numbers of working-class voters); and this they will frustrate. They will protect their real incomes, initially, by enforcing compensating claims for higher money incomes so creating a violent wage inflation, and ultimately, by using the ballot-box to elect a different and more lenient government. In a utopia (or a dictatorship) perhaps we might transfer x per cent of a near-static G.N.P. towards eight million pensioners, better housing and clearing up pollution; in the rough democratic world in which we live, we cannot.

The point is illustrated by recent experience. The transfer of resources, which a Labour Government wants, inevitably requires high taxation and public expenditure. But the popular mood is one of intense resentment of high taxation and of certain forms of public spending, such as family allowances and supplementary benefits. This mood unquestionably inhibited us from doing many of the things we wished.

Now the mood is no doubt partly due to myth and ignorance; I cannot convince any of my constituents that they are not paying a marginal (if not an average!) rate of income tax of 8s. 3d. in the pound. But it is also due to a harsh reality, the reality of slow growth. People will never like paying taxes; they all want, and reasonably so, more money to spend on themselves and their families; they like it even less when, as has been the case over the last five years, personal spending (as measured by consumption per head) has risen by little more than 1 per cent a year. This was a small enough increase anyway, and moreover, it wholly failed to match the expectations created in the 1950s when, for a variety of partly fortuitous reasons, there was a rapid and sustained increase in consumption per head. People had come to expect that this would continue. When it did not, and growth slowed down, a mood of frustration set in, which gave rise not only to the present exceptional resentment of high taxation, but also to the present exceptional pressure for higher wages. And, of course, it cost us the last election.

British experience is confirmed by experience abroad. The O.E.C.D., after studying the matter, recently concluded that, 'The growth-rate of government spending ... tends to be highest in countries where output growth is highest.' It is to the lasting credit of the Labour Government that for a considerable time it resisted this tendency, and increased the share of public expenditure in G.N.P., even though growth was slow. But more recently the trend re-asserted itself, and we reined back hard on public spending as the election grew nearer. We may now take it as a certainty that rapid growth is an essential condition of any significant re-allocation of resources. (It is also of course desirable for many other reasons.) Growth alone can give us the elbow-room we need, and remove the present dispiriting constriction on almost any form of public spending.

The Anti-growth Argument

As soon as we claim for growth a higher priority than it has had in the past, we run into some well-entrenched opposition and moreover find that some of our supporters are ill-equipped for the argument. On the one hand there is now a positive anti-growth lobby amongst the environmentalists. On the other hand, many of those who currently preach growth make it sound altogether too easy; they will the end but ignore the means.

I start with the opposition. More and more people are arguing that growth has too high a priority already, and are warning us of its costs in terms of pollution and threats to the environment. The Duke of Edinburgh remarks scathingly that 'G.N.P. is rapidly assuming the religious significance of a graven image'; anti-growth economists on both Right and Left, like Professors Mishan and Galbraith, are amongst the most revered pundits of the day; and doomwatch journalists have had the run of their lives in the last twelve months.

We must treat any argument based on the environment with instinctive sympathy and deadly seriousness. Our concern is, indeed, embodied in my fourth objective; and there are very real costs to economic growth. Higher production means more pollution of every kind, more smoke, noise, pesticides, effluent, garbage. Higher living-standards, and particularly the demand for more space and more mobility, must mean more encroachment on the countryside. Urban clearance will threaten historic buildings; urban roads will ruin existing houses; redevelopment will destroy traditional patterns of living. And these are not costs simply in terms of aristocratic amenity. Working-class people are becoming more and more concerned, from the inhabitants of Acklam Road to the millions of anglers; and one notes the growing interest of local Labour Parties in questions of the environment.

It follows that we must not become growth extremists, manically fixed on index numbers of production and seizing on any technological innovation regardless of social (or, in the case of Concorde, even economic) cost. Japan is an example of a country which, having single-mindedly pursued the goal of quantitative growth, is now counting the environmental cost and finding it extremely heavy.

Our task is to ensure that growth really does lead to an increase in welfare, remembering that welfare consists not only of the quantity of goods and services produced, but also of the quality of the environment in which they are consumed. We are therefore concerned, here as in other fields, with the quality and composition of the growth. We must continuously bring the environmental argument into the balance-sheet; and we must devote part of the growth to combating its costs.

This can be done. The technical answers to most forms of pollution are known, and, in the long run, it is possible to produce quieter aircraft-engines, pollution-free cars, clean rivers, safe pesticides and effective waste disposal. Sensible planning can conserve the countryside even in the face of more people with more cars and more leisure. And urban planning can, in theory at least, protect the urban environment; though in practice it often fails to do so owing to the low taste and filthy greed of private property developers and the unimaginative inhumanity of some local councils.

It can be done, given the will and the right priorities. It will require high public expenditure, more rigorous and imaginative planning, and an inflexible determination to impose on both industry and consumer the full costs of the pollution which they create. It will, in other words, involve (as do all our objectives) an allocation of resources which is not determined by market forces but reflects our social priorities. But none of this is an argument against the growth which we desperately need to fulfil *all* our objectives; it is an argument for discriminating growth, and for applying its fruits intelligently. To say that we must attend meticulously to the environmental case does not mean that we must go to the other extreme, and wholly neglect the economic case. Here we must beware of some of our friends. For parts of the conservationist lobby would do precisely this.

Their approach is hostile to growth in principle and indifferent to the needs of ordinary people. It has a manifest class

bias, and reflects a set of middle- and upper-class value judgments. Its champions are often kindly and dedicated people,
but they are affluent, and fundamentally, though of course not
consciously, they want to kick the ladder down behind them.
They are highly selective in their concern, being militant
mainly about threats to rural peace and wildlife and well-
loved beauty spots; they are little concerned with the far more
desperate problem of the urban environment in which 80 per
cent of our fellow citizens live.

Being ignorant of the need for growth and the plight of
ordinary people, they cannot see there is even a conflict
of interest over a reservoir on Dartmoor, potash mining in
Yorkshire, or the acquisition of rural land for over-spill housing.
The fact that Plymouth is an intermediate area with above
average unemployment, that potash mining will increase
national prosperity, that over-spill housing may relieve the
misery of thousands of slum families—these facts are not even
put into the balance-sheet. The economic argument is totally
ignored; preservation of the status quo is the sole desire.
Sometimes of course they are splendidly right, and we *should*
override the economic argument (as we did in the case of
Swincombe and as the U.S. Senate did over S.S.T.). But what
is not tolerable is to pretend that it does not exist.

At the extreme the approach becomes comical, as when
Mishan proposes towns where only horses and horse-drawn
vehicles would be admitted, and a ban on all international air
travel. No doubt such hair shirt solutions would be good for
our health; they obviously appeal to lean and fit professors.
But it is easy to see what the result would be. To quote Mishan,
'with more leisurely travel restored, one could confidently
expect an enormous reduction in the demand for foreign
travel.' Yes, indeed, the rich would proceed in leisurely fashion
across Europe to the Mediterranean beauty spots where they
would park their Rolls Royces and take to a boat or horse-
drawn vehicle. As for my constituents, who have only a fort-
night's holiday, let them eat cake and go back to Blackpool.

Now this attitude is no doubt natural, and there is probably something of it lurking in many Fabians. Affluence is obviously more agreeable when it is a minority condition. Driving round the country was much pleasanter when the roads were nearly empty. Venice and Majorca have been ruined for the minority since the *hoi polloi* invaded in their charter flights and the local peasantry bought noisy Vespas. And a rural retreat was safer and more serene, before demands for lower housing densities began to decant the urban masses into the countryside.

But of course the approach is unacceptable. My working-class constituents have their own version of the environment, which is equally valid and which calls for economic growth. They want lower housing densities and better schools and hospitals; they want washing machines and refrigerators to relieve domestic drudgery; they want cars, and the freedom they give on weekends and holidays; and they want package-tour holidays to Majorca, even if this means more noise of night flights and eating fish and chips on previously secluded beaches—why should they too not enjoy the sun? They want these things not (as Galbraith implies) because their minds have been brain-washed and their tastes contrived by advertising, but because the things are desirable in themselves. It is reasonable to argue that these consumer pleasures should take second place to more urgent social claims; it is neither reasonable nor attractive to treat them with lofty condescension and disdain. As I wrote many years ago, those enjoying an above-average standard of living should be chary of admonishing those less fortunate on the perils of material riches. For since there are many less fortunate citizens, we cannot accept a view of the environment which is essentially elitist, protectionist and anti-growth. We must make our own value judgment based on socialist objectives; and that judgment must, for the reasons I gave earlier, be that growth is vital, and that its benefits will far outweigh its costs.

In fact the anti-growth approach is not only unacceptable in terms of values; it is absurd in terms of the environment itself, however narrowly defined. For the greater part of the environmental problem stems, not from present or future growth, but from past growth. It is largely a backlog problem; the legacy of a hundred years of unplanned growth. It is a problem of *existing* slum housing, polluted rivers, derelict land and belching factories. Even if we stopped all further growth tomorrow we should still need to spend huge additional sums on coping with pollution; it will, for example, cost hundreds of millions of pounds to clean our rivers of their present pollution. My previous argument applies here also. We have no chance of finding these huge sums from a near-static G.N.P., any more than we could find the extra sums we want for health or education or any of our other goals. Only rapid growth will give us any possibility.

The Conditions of Faster Growth

So the case for growth remains unshaken; not growth at any cost, but certainly growth much faster than the 2 per cent of recent years. How can a future Labour Government achieve this?

The low growth-rate has two causes. First, British productivity rises more slowly than that of other countries, so that even if it grew to its full productive potential (say 3½ per cent per annum) it would still be a slow-growing nation by European standards. There are endless conflicting theories to explain this phenomenon, ranging from the imperial background through the public school system to a faulty structure of industry. The fact that our own policies for higher productivity, with all their brave talk about technology, restructuring and economies of scale, had only a limited success, should teach us some humility. Nobody can claim to know the answer, and there is manifestly no short-term panacea.

The second cause lies in the all too successful efforts of postwar British Governments to hold down growth even *below* the productive potential. This they have done because changes in home demand—crudely, stop-go and deflation—have been used as the main instrument for controlling (or attempting to control) the balance of payments and the level of inflation.

One can see why this happened. Alternative instruments, such as devaluation or incomes policy, seemed fraught with difficulties: the pound's role as a world currency, the existence of the sterling balances, the pressure of the United States and other monetary authorities, traditions of free collective bargaining and so on. And when the Labour Government finally did devalue in 1967, and removed the constraint on growth of an over-valued pound, we found that we had not rid ourselves of the other constraint, inflation. So having first curtailed growth in the interests of the balance of payments, it is now curtailed in the interests of greater price stability. On existing policies growth will continue to be sacrificed to one or other of these two objectives.

A future Labour Government must therefore consciously alter the priorities. This requires a *political* decision. Economists and Treasury officials can list the various objectives of economic policy: growth, full employment, stable prices and a healthy foreign balance. But when these conflict, as they almost always do, it is for politicians to decide the priorities. Governments since the war have dithered and wavered between the objectives, hoping that something would turn up miraculously to reconcile them; in the last resort the balance of payments usually had priority, so that when people spoke of the economy being weak or strong they were assumed to be referring to the foreign balance. But with the mounting price which low growth exacts from the British people, I am clear that we must in the future alter the priorities in favour of economic growth.

This is easy to say, especially in opposition. We said it loudly in 1963-4; and many are saying it again today as though the last six years had never existed. But there is neither point nor honesty in preaching growth unless we accept, as we did not in those six years, the necessary corollaries. If we are not to use changes in home demand to regulate the balance of payments and price inflation, we must have other instruments for the purpose and be prepared to use them.

This means, firstly, a greater flexibility of exchange rates. I am not speaking of a floating rate, but of a willingness to make timely adjustments to the parity, whenever the alternative would be serious deflation. This after all was Keynes's intention at Bretton Woods. It was for years frustrated by financial orthodoxy, false morality and a Cromer-style anthropomorphic worship of the pound sterling. The atmosphere is now much more propitious. It is clear to everyone that the recent changes in the British, French and German parities have improved the world monetary situation out of all recognition. Today the I.M.F., backed by a growing weight of outside opinion, talks openly of exchange-rate adjustment as an indispensable part of economic policy. I only hope that the Labour Party, having paid so heavy a price for clinging to the opposite view from 1964 to 1967, has now learned this lesson.

Secondly, inflation. This is currently proceeding at the rate of 7 per cent per annum. It is no comfort that other O.E.C.D. countries are in the same boat; they at least (with the exception of the United States) have the compensation, which we do not, of rapid growth. In any case their inflation is more likely to slow down than ours. No British Government could endure indefinitely a 7 per cent rate of inflation. Apart from the appalling social effects, the voters will not put up with it; and the Government's majority would rapidly crumble away at by-elections. If there is no *alternative* method of dealing with it, then squeeze and deflation will follow as night follows day. No doubt, for political reasons, they will be used half-heartedly; and there is no guarantee that they will be successful. But bitter experience shows that even a half-hearted and only partially successful squeeze can cause an intolerable loss of output and employment. The only alternative, that is if the country really *wants* sustained growth, is a prices and incomes policy; and this has to be faced. Would that it were not so! For successive British Governments have tried almost every conceivable version of such a policy, from Crippsian exhortation (oddly, the most successful) through guide-lines and early warning to legislation and freeze; and we are now back to square one. Nor has any other country done much better. Yet the O.E.C.D. is surely right when it says that,

> The success of incomes policies has so far been limited. But the alternatives may prove unworkable or unacceptable. It therefore appears highly desirable, and probably inevitable, that the search should go on; and it would be wrong to underestimate the possibilities of progress.

No progress will be made under the present Government, even if it had not contracted out of the search. For the unions cannot be expected to co-operate against a background of stagnation and unemployment; and the prospective battle over the Industrial Relations Bill must in any case rule out any constructive dialogue for a long period ahead.

But Labour in opposition, having explicitly committed itself to growth, must attempt the search. There will be opposition from some, though by no means all, trade union leaders. But we must remember that the unions and the Party have their own distinct fields of responsibility, and their own distinct duties and obligations to their members and electors; neither is, nor should be, the creature of the other. The Labour Party is a broad-based, national, people's party: it must not be deterred from finding national solutions to national problems. Yet the area of mutual need and common interest is, and always has been, enormous; and a prices and incomes policy will surely prove to fall within it. Neither Party nor unions can attain their goals without continuous growth; and we shall not achieve that growth without an incomes policy. The stark alternative is periodic bouts of deflation and unemployment. This surely provides a sufficient imperative to talks between the Party and the unions. And by this I do not mean merely hearty back-slapping and cheerful cameraderie which avoids the awkward issues. I mean serious discussion designed to lead to a practical solution.

Taxation and Social Control

We want faster growth the better and more quickly to attain our four objectives—the elimination of poverty, a greater equality of wealth, a civilized standard of social provision, and the improvement of our environment. But growth will not, as I have pointed out, automatically produce the allocation of resources required for these objectives, though it will greatly help. Only government can produce that allocation; and the essential means to doing so are higher public spending and greater social control. Here we face a difficulty, for not only are these anathema to the Tories—indeed, they have never been anathematized with a more manic and ideological fervour than recently by Mr Heath—but they are by no means popular with the British public.

Take taxation and public expenditure, on which I feel I have shouted myself hoarse over the years. Within any given country, this is an issue between Left and Right. But when one makes comparisons *between* countries one finds that other factors, notably the cultural tradition of the country concerned, are also a potent influence.

It is true that in nearly all advanced countries public expenditure has long been rising faster than total output, probably since the turn of the century, with the main pressure coming from education, health and welfare services. With the changing age-structure of the population, the insistent demand for higher standards and the growing concern with urban congestion and renewal, it is certain that the pressure will continue.

But different countries react to the pressure differently. Contrary to popular belief, Britain has certainly not taken on the largest public burden. Five of the fourteen countries belonging to the O.E.C.D. have a higher burden of taxation than Britain. The share of public expenditure in G.N.P. is lower in Britain than in Germany, France, Sweden, Holland, Norway and Austria. The share of private consumption in G.N.P. is appreciably higher in Britain than in all the faster growing industralized countries. And what is significant is that the ranking of countries in these matters depends as much on their cultural tradition as on whether their governments are Left or Right.

Similarly with social control. There will have to be more regulation as society grows more complex and interdependent. Pollution is a case in point, which will call for an increasing degree of bureaucratic and institutional control, if we are to contain it. Mr Heath's philosophy of laissez-faire and passive government is grotesquely irrelevant in this day and age; and as for Mr Rubin and his Yippies, their philosophy of 'down with detail and bureaucracy, let everyone do his own thing,' is a sure way of abruptly bringing civilization to an end.

Thus there will have to be more, not less, control over industry, as firms become larger, more complex and more international—in the interests of regional equality, environmental planning, anti-pollution and consumer protection. As population and living-standards rise, there will have to be more, not less, control over the use of land, firmer local authority structure-plans to shape the changing urban environment, ambitious regional plans like the South-East study to deal with the problem of the conurbations, and new and imaginative plans to control and relieve the pressures on the countryside. The more that the environment matters, the more government action will be needed; for, as Samuel Lubell once remarked, 'Only God can create a tree, but only Government can create a park.' Certainly God alone cannot create an Alkali Inspectorate or stop the barbaric depredations of profit-hungry property firms. And there will have to be more social control over individuals, over where they can take their cars, or build their houses or dispose of their garbage and litter.

Now, as far as certain of these things are concerned, this country's record compares well with that of other countries, but if one takes the whole field of taxation, public expenditure, social control and collective responsibility—all the essential means to attaining our objectives—then cultural attitudes in Britain are by no means favourable to us.

I quote the following passage from *The Conservative Enemy*, written nearly a decade ago:

A Protestant country, and the first to embrace capitalism, we retain a tradition (though now weakened) of self-help and individualism, of free enterprise and Manchester Liberalism, and hence an antipathy to government or civic action and collective welfare. A materialist country, we rate private commercial success exceptionally high, and the public servant (along with the intellectual, the artist and the churchman) exceptionally low; hence private outlays are considered fruitful and social outlays wasteful. A hierarchial country, we have a bourgeoisie which has always (notably in education) made private provision for its own collective services; and the public communal services have been correspondingly neglected. A socially divided country, we lack a sense of community; the middle classes, ignorant of how the other half lives, retain a 'coals in the bath' attitude, believing the working classes to be lazy and feckless and pampered by the Welfare State; hence a further bias against social spending. A philistine country, we care little for the arts or for creative urban planning; so we spend less on art patronage or amenities than any civilized country in the world. An insular and unimaginative country, we have exceptionally low cultural expectations and show an extraordinary passivity in the face of squalor and discomfort; hence we endure without protest disgraceful conditions in hospitals, trains or rural schools (as we do in shops and restaurants). These lingering national traits, although one hopes they are gradually fading, make it harder to redress the imbalance.

There have been some obvious improvements since I wrote that, mainly due to the actions of the Labour Government, but much of the passage would stand today. Indeed at this very moment foreign opinion boggles, with a mixture of pity and disbelief, at a country which can so vulgarly, and with so little public protest, dismantle its Consumer Council. Since we have these public attitudes to contend with, as well as bitter party opposition from the Tories, it is surely obvious that to carry through a radical, egalitarian programme, involving a major redistribution of resources, is a most formidable task which will absorb all our energies for many years to come.

False Trails

Yet at this very moment we hear the siren voices of some left-wing publicists, both in this country and the United States, urging us to gallop off in a totally different direction. They concede that the basic issues are still of some importance, but, having made that quick obeisance, they go on to say that the real issues of the 1970s will be quite different ones, alienation, communication, participation, automation, dehumanization, decentralization, the information network, student revolt, the generation gap or even Women's Lib. Now no doubt these polysyllables all conceal an important truth, even though I cannot myself discern it in every case, and occasionally dislike what I can discern. For example, I find much of the talk of the generation gap both distasteful and inaccurate. It is distasteful, because it often goes with a self-abasing attitude towards youth as a class, and even youthful violence, as something to be compared flatteringly with the old effete Parliamentary system. It reminds me of the cult of youth that was celebrated so odiously in the Fascist hymn 'Giovenezza'. For myself, I believe that no generation should abase itself before another — neither young before old, nor old before young; and I believe profoundly in a non-violent Parliamentary system, even an imperfect one like ours.

As to accuracy, most of those who talk and write about the generation gap, are referring in fact to a small minority of students. They ignore the overwhelming evidence of opinion polls and attitude surveys which show, for example, that the great majority of the 18–24 age-group vote as their parents do. Of course there is, always has been, and always will be, a generation gap; and of course there is a student revolt (in some sense) with the vast expansion of student numbers, and a revolt that has probably on balance done good. But one should keep the matter in some perspective. S. M. Lipset and Earl Raab, who have done the most exhaustive survey of all the poll material on this subject in the United States, come to the following conclusion. One may like it or one may not, but at least it is based on the best information that can be assembled. 'Politically, at least, the significant fact is that the basic direction of the younger generation is in most cases the same as that of their parents; they go with the parental grain rather than against it.'

However, that is a digression. My main point is that the new NWI formulations must not be allowed to divert us from the overwhelmingly more important issues which I have talked about in this lecture. To illustrate my point, I will discuss, briefly, the most significant and sympathetic, though still somewhat vague and hardly new, of these formulations: namely, participation.

Participation, I suppose, should mean that the general public participates directly in decision-making, and not just indirectly, through its elected representatives. It is an ideal of Athenian democracy, to be realized through the medium of the mass meeting or the strictly local forum.

Now in a society as large and complex as ours, participation of this kind can occur only on a limited scale. It can occur in the case of a strike, or a particular local planning decision, but there is no way in which the general public can participate directly in the South-East Planning Study, or the Roskill Commission, or the G.L.C. Development Plan, any more than the bulk of workers can participate in the investment decisions of I.C.I. or the British Steel Corporation. In any case, experience shows that only a small minority of the population wish to participate in this way. I repeat what I have often said: the majority prefer to lead a full family life and cultivate their gardens. And a good thing too, for if we believe in socialism as a means of increasing personal freedom and the range of choice, we do not necessarily want a busy bustling society in which everyone is politically active, and fussing around in an interfering and responsible manner, and herding us all into participating groups. The threat to privacy and freedom would be intolerable; moreover, as Bertrand Russell once wrote, 'The sphere of individual action is not to be regarded as ethically inferior to that of social duty.'

In fact, what I am talking about is usually something different, namely, voluntary pressure-groups of one kind or another. These exist to exert pressure from the outside, rather than to participate from the inside. They are either groups representing consumers of the products of industry or government, such as the Consumer Association, CASE, or the Patients' Association; or they are part of the conservation or environmental lobby, whether on a national scale like the Civic Trust and C.P.R.E. or on a local scale to fight a Stansted or a motorway or a reservoir; or they exist to promote a particular social cause, like Shelter and the C.P.A.G.; or—and these in particular I shall revert to later—they take the form of community or neighbourhood associations.

These voluntary and pressure-group activities have grown spectacularly in recent years. For my part, I have been energetically involved in many of them, and have no doubt that they are on balance an enormous force for good. They provide a badly needed element of countervailing power in our society; and I would like to see them extend and strengthen their activities, for example, in many of the directions in which Ralph Nader has led the American consumer movement. This would, by the way, be a less trivial outlet for the idealism of young activists than throwing smoke bombs at Miss World.

But I said 'on balance' an enormous force for good; and I must stress that these activities are not necessarily *socialist* in either content or intention. Many of the groups are basically middle class, or even (in the case of some conservation groups) upper class, or even (in the case of the World Wildlife Fund) Princely or Royal in membership and origin! Now when the interests of different classes coincide, as with protecting the consumer, or getting better schools, or preserving the coastline, or where the object is plainly to help the under-privileged as with Shelter and the C.P.A.G. this may not matter. But in other cases it does matter. I have already pointed to the elitist tendencies in parts of the rural conservation movement. Some urban amenity groups are having the effect, in areas of acute housing shortage, of diminishing the supply of working-class housing in the interests of the middle class. There are risks even in education. The voluntary playgroup movement, for example, which I strongly support, could be widening the gap between privileged and under-privileged children; while the demand from some CASE branches for more parental influence in the schools could easily in practice impose an even more middle-class ethos on the schools than they have today. There are times when only the despised local councillors and bureaucrats stand guard on behalf of the majority.

I conclude two things from this. Firstly, although we should remain ardent supporters of most of these voluntary activities, we should be discriminating in our support and not automatically equate this kind of participation with socialism; Tories can participate as actively as Socialists. Secondly, we must seek ways of involving the majority in what is so far largely a minority movement; and I revert here to the concept of the neighbourhood or community council.

Apart from major decisions of central government, the decisions which most affect most people's lives are decisions about their locality—about particular roads, particular schools, particular housing estates, particular factories. They are decisions about a motorway route, the exact date of clearance of a slum street, play areas on a housing estate, the smell from a new factory, a new twenty-storey hotel in a quiet residential area, the disappearance of small shopkeepers under town centre redevelopment, and whether lorries should park in a residential street. It is not only a matter of stopping things. People in a locality may also want to *do* things—to spend money on local amenities, such as a car park, a playing field or old people's benches, and to make appointments to school governing bodies and other local bodies. It is at this local level that people often feel most helpless in the face of authority. They do not want a continuous process of active participation, but they do want to be consulted about, and to influence, these decisions which profoundly affect their daily lives. Precisely the same is of course true in industry, and constitutes the essence of industrial democracy.

Large local government units—and they will become larger whatever form of local government reorganization is decided upon—do not always practice such consultation effectively. True, one-purpose pressure-groups may spring up to challenge a particular decision; but they often prove ephemeral. That is why, in the February 1970 White Paper on Local Government Reform, I tried to give an impetus to the idea of smaller local or neighbourhood councils—urban parish councils, so to speak; and Michael Young and his colleagues on the Association of Neighbourhood Councils have pushed the idea still further.

Naturally the idea evokes both scepticism and hostility. Some, especially though not only amongst officials, see such councils as a potential threat to good administration—yet another irritating pressure-group getting in the way of sound government. Others think them simply absurd, as did all the respectable, established people in G. K. Chesterton's *The Napoleon of Notting Hill*. I do not know how many Fabians remember that novel, but it is worth recalling, perhaps, the answer given by Adam Wayne, the Provost of Notting Hill (where I am happy to live). He was asked by the King,

> 'Don't you really think the sacred Notting Hill at all absurd?'
> 'Absurd?' asked Wayne, blankly, 'Why should I? Notting Hill,' said the Provost simply, 'is a rise or high ground of the common earth, on which men have built houses to live, in which they are born, fall in love, pray, marry and die. Why should I think it absurd?'

Whether absurd or not, and I doubt if it is, this much is clear. In an age of increasingly and inevitably larger units, there is both a no doubt inchoate, but very real, discontent with the channels open to people to influence events, and also a growing interest in specifically neighbourhood and community action. This is surely something we should encourage; and the neighbourhood council opens up a way forward, which we should boldly take, even in advance of legislation. It seems most suitable that the first experiment is currently being tried in the Golborne Ward of Notting Hill.

Conclusion

But even such a challenging idea as this, still less the ambiguous though fashionable formulations I mentioned earlier, must not be allowed to divert us too far from our central objectives.

It would, for a start, be electorally idiotic to be so diverted. We can learn a lesson from American experience last summer and autumn, when the 'New Politics' section of the Democratic

Party tried, even to the extent of opposing excellent liberal candidates in the primaries, to move the Democrats away from their traditional support in the working class and ethnic groups, towards an essentially middle-class orientation and set of issues. It was only when the Democrats reverted in the autumn to the central economic issues that they were able—with remarkable success—to fight off an immensely strong Republican offensive in the mid-term elections.

It would not only be electorally unwise; more important, it would be wrong. I have always looked forward, in everything which I have written, to the day when we could stop fussing about growth and the allocation of resources, and turn our attention to more fruitful and cultural pursuits. But that day is not here yet. The basic issues of poverty, inequality, an inadequate social sector and a drab environment are still the overriding ones; and questions of growth, taxation, expenditure and social control remain incomparably more urgent than alienation or student revolt or the mass media. And that is not to mention the impoverished condition of the developing countries.

If there were some who doubted this on June 18th, they surely cannot do so now. The new Conservative Government is showing itself the most ideological and reactionary right-wing government that Europe has seen in two decades. It cannot eliminate poverty, for that would involve more generous public spending. It believes in inequality; hence Mr Barber's mini-budget redistributes income from the less well-off to the better-off, and Mrs Thatcher's Circular 10/70 reduces equality in education. It believes in the greatest possible freedom for private profit making; so it abolishes I.R.C., transfers assets from B.O.A.C. to the private sector, and talks of the need for general denationalization. It shows its contempt for the consumer by abolishing the Consumer Council. It threatens the regions by its policy on investment grants, and the cities by relaxing controls on speculative office building. Its commitment to lower public spending and its ideology of laissez-faire will mean more poverty, more inequality, a meaner social sector and a worse environment.

Perhaps it did not need this lecture to demonstrate that our basic social-democratic aims remain as urgent as they have ever been. If proof were needed, Mr Heath has provided it.

Postscript: A Riposte to Galbraith

The publication of A Social-Democratic Britain *provoked a correspondence in the columns of the* New Statesman *on the importance of economic growth, to which Professor J. K. Galbraith, author of* The Affluent Society, *contributed, on January 22nd, 1971, an article entitled 'Galbraith Answers Crosland'. Anthony Crosland's reply, reproduced here, was published in the* New Statesman *on January 28th, 1971.*

Sir,

Professor Galbraith makes the following points in reply to my Fabian pamphlet.

Firstly, he states that I am 'merely silly'. I have thought closely about this, while in my bath, but do not really see what, at my age, I can do to cure this distressing disability.

Secondly, he appears to be arguing that, contrary to popular impression, he is not really anti-growth at all. I confess I find this hard to square with his recent interview in the *Observer*, when he said that 'we should expect, even hope for, a slower rate of economic growth.' My poor, poor country—slower even than the 2 per cent of recent years!

Thirdly, he chides me for accepting the need for an incomes policy only 'with the enhanced vision which comes to all of us when we are out of office'. This seems a little uncomradely, since I was for six years a loyal member of a government which tried almost every conceivable form of incomes policy.

Fourthly, he makes the bizarre assertion that, 'overwhelmingly it is the production and consumption of the well-to-do and rich which cause the trouble' (of environmental pollution). This must surely be an example of the famous Galbraith humour. Motor cars? Night charter flights? Waste and refuse? Reservoirs? Polluting factories? Oil on the beaches? Let us march forward together, the professor and I, to attack the well-to-do and rich—but surely we cannot blame them alone for pollution.

Lastly, he argues that economic growth by itself is not enough; what matters is how it is distributed. This is precisely the message of my Fabian pamphlet.

Some of your other correspondents seem to have misunderstood my basic position, so perhaps you will allow me briefly to restate it. I am, and always have been, a passionate supporter of most conservation and environmental causes. As a minister I was privileged to play some part in stopping Stansted, reprieving Richmond Terrace and Norman Shaw's Scotland Yard, setting up a uniquely thorough inquiry into a G.L.C.'s motorway proposals, establishing a Royal Commission on environmental pollution, and publishing the first-ever comprehensive White Paper on the subject.

But I also believe that some sections of the environmental lobby are basically hostile to economic growth and indifferent to the needs of ordinary people, and that this attitude is (a) morally wrong when we still have so many pressing social needs, and (b) self-defeating since without growth we shall never find the huge sums of money which we desperately need to cure pollution and improve the environment.

ANTHONY CROSLAND

4 *Labour and 'Populism'*

Originally published in the Sunday Times *on April 4th, 1971.*

When at midnight on March 24th Mr Pym gave his ebullient shout of 'Aye' to the Third Reading of the Industrial Relations Bill, it marked the beginning of the end of the first phase of opposition in this Parliament. The Budget will prolong the phase for some time yet. But it is clear that Labour must soon embark on the second phase.

Up to now, Opposition tactics have inevitably been dictated by the actions of the Government. Since the Tory General Election victory on June 18th last year, new policy statements have poured out in rapid succession, on comprehensive education, housing finance, social charges, regional policy, denationalization, South African arms, industrial relations and now the Budget. These have been not only reactionary in content, but couched in more provocatively right-wing language than we have heard since the 1930s.

The Labour Party reacted with a united fury; and it has rightly concentrated on instant Parliamentary opposition. There has been no recurrence of the doctrinal strife which rent the party after 1951 and 1959. Instead, we have witnessed a highly disciplined, determined and cohesive Parliamentary Opposition.

This must and will continue; it constitutes the first duty of an Opposition. But from now on it must not be Labour's *sole* preoccupation; for by itself it will not be enough. For one thing, we cannot rely on the Government to hang itself. As we move steadily towards the middle of the Parliament, and by-election results may begin to send shivers of anxiety through the Tory benches, even Mr Heath's Government will move unobtrusively towards the centre, and instant opposition will not then yield the dividends it does today.

Moreover, while the voters will swing away from the Tories, they may swing not to Labour, but to abstention. It is less than a year since Labour lost the election, with its lowest share of the poll since 1935. Large numbers of its potential supporters drifted away. However unpopular the Tories, these voters will want positive reasons for returning to the Party which they deserted last June. They will not be satisfied with being referred back to the achievement of 1964–70, for it was precisely that achievement which they found inadequate. They will want to know what we stand for now. We shall be asked for our credentials.

I am not suggesting that we should immediately publish a series of detailed policy statements (though we should certainly initiate a *long-term* programme of work on future policy). But increasingly the voters will want to know what sort of a party we are and what are our basic objectives.

We cannot go back to the 1964 image of technology and managerialism—the D.E.A./aluminium smelter syndrome; it would scarcely carry conviction after six years of growth at 2 per cent. Nor can we revert to the stance of last June—bashing the Tories but silent about our own policies; the voters showed in their last-minute switch to the Tories that they were interested in real issues and wanted a party with a clear identity.

I have given my own views in my Fabian pamphlet *A Social-Democratic Britain*. I believe that a left-wing party's priorities are firstly to relieve misery wherever it exists—to help the deprived, the poor and the underdogs; secondly, to promote a greater social and economic equality for the mass of the people; thirdly, to apply strict social control to the economic system in the interests of the environment, the consumer and the less prosperous regions.

These objectives, which are in Labour's central tradition of conscience and reform, call for a reallocation of resources and a redistribution of wealth. They require high taxation and public expenditure and rigorous government controls. This is the basic divide between Left and Right; a divide which a Tory Government is now joyously revealing.

The authors of an important new Fabian pamphlet,[1] however, argue that the modern Labour Party does not wholly live up to its central traditions and that the basic divide became badly blurred during the years of 'responsible' Labour Government. Labour's major achievements, they argue, were not in the field of social and economic equality, but in that of individual freedom—the relaxation of censorship, greater tolerance in matters of sex, reform of the divorce laws, penal reforms, the appointment of an ombudsman and so on. There were, of course, also measures of economic interventionism, social welfare and educational advance. But compared with the amount of 'socialist-liberal' reform, there was only moderate progress towards reducing the major inequalities with which socialists have been traditionally concerned.

This elevation of liberal reform to such a prominent place makes a strong appeal to the radical middle class, to whom issues of morality, culture and personal expression, are often more important than the hard, patient slog of social reform. But it carries a risk of loss of working-class support. A predominantly middle-class leadership with these liberal preoccupations may come to neglect the more traditional issues, which are the primary concern of ordinary Labour voters; and these voters may cease to turn to Labour for the redress of their grievances. Messrs Gyford and Haseler refer to

the sense of estrangement felt by many working-class voters towards a government whose policies sometimes seemed to bear little relation to the realities of the everyday life of ordinary people, and whose concern for permissive legislation, the arts, higher education and technological efficiency could not mask its failure to deal adequately with housing, unemployment and the cost of living.

In short, these authors argue, there are two strands in modern socialism—'liberal-progressivism' and 'Labourist-populism'; and the first has dangerously overlaid the second.

Now, although they overstate their argument, I have a profound sympathy with its general drift. But first one must decide what Labourist-populism does not mean.

Firstly it does not mean that the Labour Party should identify itself with every militant trade union leader and every strike and every wage-claim. To be so identified would, ironically, cut us off from a huge section of working-class and trade union opinion—that moderate opinion which is so clearly uneasy about extreme militancy, continual strikes and uncontrolled inflation. It is represented at the top by Mr Victor Feather and many others; and it is becoming increasingly manifest at the grass-roots level of the rank-and-file (whose views are dubiously represented by some of the militant block-votes cast on their behalf at conferences).

Moreover such an identification would give sanction to a wholly unacceptable distribution of income. For in a free-for-all, airline pilots (already paid more than Cabinet Ministers) and doctors come out top, Mr Clive Jenkins's members second, car workers a good third, postal workers and railwaymen a bad fourth, and the really poor nowhere. Competitive militancy wins the most for the best-organized and higher-paid; the strong become stronger and the weak become weaker, as after a Tory Budget. That is one (though not the only) reason why Labour must stand adamantly for an incomes policy.

Secondly, 'populism' does not mean that we must follow every whim and fad of public prejudice and intolerance. We must heed the fate of American Populism. Beginning in the 1890s as an idealistic reform movement, on behalf of the underdog against big business, the railroads and the trusts, and associated with the heroic figures of the young William Jennings Bryan, and the Progressive La Follette, it gradually turned sour. It developed a violent antipathy to parliamentary democracy and a mystical belief in the direct democracy of the

mass meeting and the referendum; and by the 1930s it had
degenerated into the xenophobic, anti-semitic, authoritarian
demagogy of Huey Long and Father Coughlin.

In Britain today, a populist approach, if one takes the term
literally, would mean the restoration of hanging and flogging,
a Powellite policy on race, vast reductions in income tax, the
withdrawal of family allowances, and an end to student grants
and overseas aid. Without arguing the age-old question of
how far government is entitled to defy the wishes of the
voters, I state flatly that such policies are unacceptable to any
Social Democrat.

Messrs Gyford and Haseler are not, however, arguing that
the Labour Party should slavishly follow public opinion, but
only that it should show a primary concern for those social and
economic issues which most affect ordinary working-class
people (white-collar as well as manual). They are urging on us
a certain attitude of mind, a particular set of priorities for our
attention.

I agree with them. I have long been locked in conflict with
a middle-class element on the Left which seems to me to show
an elitist and even condescending attitude to the wants and
aspirations of ordinary people. (This elitism is notably strong
among violently 'radical' students in the universities.) Incredible as it may seem, I and others have had to defend the affluent
society and the right of the workers to own motor cars and
take packaged holidays. I have recently had to criticize some
of my friends in the environmental lobby for not realizing
that 80 per cent of our people live an urban life. And while I
think it wholly right to debate the Rudi Dutschke case, I
would think it even more important to debate housing or
education.

The need for a populist streak in our thinking becomes
greater as the social composition of the Parliamentary Labour
Party changes and college graduates (and often lecturers)
increasingly outnumber trade union M.P.s. The temptation
becomes ever stronger to seek the esteem of the liberal audience

of columnists and television commentators, college graduates also, with essentially middle-class values, who since childhood, have seldom ventured out of the introverted world of central London into the rougher provincial world where most Labour voters live. When I was Minister of Education, five times as many Labour M.P.s attended a debate on overseas students' fees as ever attended debates on primary schools. This cannot be right.

There are also electoral consequences. The forthcoming Nuffield study of the 1970 General Election[2] suggests that the swing against Labour was highest among unskilled workers and the poor. This is of course largely to be explained by Labour's deflationary policies and the failure of the standard of living to rise in line with expectations. But it may also be partly due to 'the sense of estrangement', felt by many work-ing-class voters. Certainly little was heard last June about comprehensive education or working-class housing or the needs of the poor. It seems incredible that we did not make a major issue of comprehensives.

To say that Labour must pay more attention to issues of popular concern is not of course to argue for abandoning issues of morality and culture. It is a matter of balance. The liberal-progressive policies, all of which I strongly support, are of deep importance and will become still more so as general living-standards rise. For myself, I have in particular a heavy emotional commitment to the question of the environment, even though I assert unfashionably that there are often two sides to the argument.

The Scandinavian Socialist Parties show that the two strands can be successfully combined. For while they have been notably active in the fields of personal freedom and culture, they have also laid the greatest stress on equality, educational reform, the welfare system and rising living-standards.

But in Britain the balance needs to be redressed. As we seek to re-create a sense of Labour's identity—other than as a Party of negative opposition, necessary though that also is—we want a shift of emphasis to the basic social issues: housing, education, social welfare, urban living, the distribution of wealth and economic growth. These are the issues which my working-class constituents want to see at the top of our agenda; they are also the issues which are central to Labour's long-term aims.

5 Preparing for the Next Election

Originally published in the Observer *on January 21st, 1973.*

'Oppositions don't win elections, Governments lose them.' If the familiar saw were true, how would we assess Labour's chances half-way through this Parliament?

On the one hand, the Government have, predictably, moved towards the centre; the era of confrontation (or what Mr Maudling euphemistically calls 'over-correction') is past, and we are back to a Macmillan-style Toryism.

This no doubt leaves Mr Heath open to the charge of blatant inconsistency; but it also greatly improves his electoral chances. To take one example, the Government's partial climb-down on 'fair rents' will take much of the angry heat out of the tenants' protest movement.

The British economy, on the other hand, is as usual heading for a crisis, which may well coincide with the next election. After a period of rising consumption and falling unemployment, Mr Heath's 5 per cent growth target seems likely to generate an overseas deficit of staggering proportions, requiring a further devaluation and all the familiar paraphernalia of deflation—higher taxation, a squeeze on consumption and the rest.

Meanwhile, despite the ambitious intentions of Phase II, the rise in food prices, now a dominant feature of the British social scene, appears certain to continue and bear harshly on the ordinary wage-earner. Indeed, the British economy shows signs of becoming an unmanageable horse which throws every successive rider. Perhaps no Government these days can last more than a single term.

Perhaps, but it would be idiotic as well as immoral for the Labour Party to rely on it. For Oppositions *can* lose elections. Even if voters turn against the Government, they may swing not to Labour but to the 'third party' of Liberals, fringe candidates or abstention.

The by-election results at Rochdale, Sutton and Uxbridge show the danger; and the polls reveal a smaller swing to Labour than would be expected after two and a half years of Mr Heath's abrasive policies. We cannot simply watch and wait and pray for the pendulum to swing or the economic crisis to develop.

The crux is that, after two years of necessary but negative Tory-bashing, the voters know what we are against but not what we are for.

It is not the case, as it was some time ago, that we have no policies for the future; *Labour's Programme for Britain* was a comparatively detailed document. True, some of the policies are largely negative, consisting mainly of repealing this and that; and they are of course of varying quality— inevitably so, given the limited financial resources available to the Party.

But the trouble goes deeper. First, we lack a clear *identity* as a party. In particular, the public does not know whether we are, or are not, the political wing of the trade union movement. Now the McGovern debacle dramatized the appalling danger to a left-wing party of neglecting its traditional working-class supporters in the interests of a largely middle-class 'New Politics' appeal.

Labour's special link is, and must be, with the organized working class, and its solid base is in the trade union movement. Both party and unions represent the same aspirations of their members and their families; and the area of common interest and mutual need is, and always will be, enormous.

But that does not mean a *complete* identity of interest. Labour is not a sectional or one-class Party, nor did most of the pioneers see it as such. They saw it rather as the party of the ordinary people against the rich, the privileged and the powerful.

Trade union leaders, whether moderate or militant, are elected by neither so large nor so representative a constituency as Prime Ministers; and while they faithfully reflect their rank-and-file members' views on matters of collective bargaining, they may not invariably reflect them on wider political issues — indeed, in the case of Mr Hugh Scanlon and a minority of extreme left-wing leaders they clearly do not.

The Labour Party should not automatically agree with everything that union leaders say, still less be dictated to by them. For all our special links with the unions, we are a national party, responsible to the people as a whole. If we are thought, as we sometimes are, to be the creature of the unions and exclusively identified with them, then Mr Heath could occupy No. 10 for a long, long time.

Secondly, we lack credibility on the central and dominant *economic* issues of the day. On inflation, Mr Heath, having started by deliberately making the problem worse, at least appears to be grappling with it now; meanwhile Labour, while it has many excellent things to say about prices, lacks any policy for incomes.

On public expenditure, for all the ritual disclaimers that we cannot do everything at once, we display a marked insouciance in public speeches and statements; we have laid down no clear priorities, and made little attempt to educate the public on the inevitable cost in taxation of the social programmes we want to see.

Underlying all is the issue of economic growth; if we have no better ideas than we had last time we shall certainly gladden the hearts of anti-growth ecologists, but we should then be chary of making promises. It is not that there are easy answers to these problems; but at least, to carry conviction, we must show ourselves publicly and candidly aware of their existence.

Thirdly, we must show ourselves more sensitive to legitimate popular grievances. I take an obvious, though controversial, example. In retrospect, the most significant feature of the Rochdale and Uxbridge by-elections may turn out to be the high votes given to anti-immigration candidates. Many, and probably most, of these came from traditional Labour supporters.

The instinctive reaction is to condemn these voters as hopelessly and repulsively racist; and no doubt there is a small such element. But it seems highly implausible that 10 per cent of the traditionally tolerant British people, and the many more who clearly sympathize with them, have suddenly embraced a racialist philosophy or succumbed to crude racial hatred. Politicians know perfectly well from their constituency contacts that this is not the case. If it were, we should have far more racial violence than we have.

The true explanation is both more plausible and more charitable. Large sections of our working people have real grievances which they believe to be intensified by continued immigration. Where there is a desperate shortage of housing for young people, and jobs are scarce, and schools already under strain, the priority given to new immigrants inevitably causes dismay. And people of an older generation, who have spent their lives in a close-knit working-class community, inevitably feel bitter when they find the local pub or cinema or corner-shop taken over by a different community with an unfamiliar culture.

To condemn such feelings as racialist is libellous and impertinent. They reflect a genuine sense of insecurity, and anxiety for a traditional way of life. I believe that the decision to admit the Ugandan Asians was morally right; but it was presented to the public in a deeply insensitive manner. The homeless and jobless of Britain are only demanding parity of compassion with homeless and jobless immigrants; and their demand is legitimate.

Politicians should not follow every whim of public prejudice, reasonable or otherwise; they must lead. But they must listen first. For if our working-class constituents come to believe

that nobody 'up there' is listening, and that the Labour leadership is remote and indifferent to what is happening in their
daily lives, then the resultant drift to Powellite extremism
would threaten not only the Labour Party, not only good race
relations, but the whole parliamentary system.

Lastly, the detailed policies which we are gradually acquiring
do not appear to be informed by a coherent vision of the society
we want to see. Last year's programme seemed rather a
collection of bits and pieces, with more emphasis on means
than ends.

It contained numerous proposals for new agencies and
boards and corporations, for changes in industrial structure,
for a new machinery of government. But it was not always
clear what this flurry of activity was intended to achieve, nor
why it should be more effective than the similar flurry after
1964.

The essential socialist objectives are greater equality, and a
more classless society; these should be the central theme of
any Labour manifesto. Some limited progress was made
towards these objectives under the Labour Government. On
present evidence, it appears that there was some diminution of
inequality of incomes after taxes and benefits, and probably
also in the field of wealth; and a good deal of progress was
made in reducing regional disparities and improving the
relative standards of the less well-off in housing and education.

But gross economic inequalities remain, and have been made
much worse by Mr Heath; and socially we remain the most
class-ridden country in the world. Labour needs detailed
egalitarian policies, most of which have already been spelled out
at different times. But still more it needs a determination to
'bash the rich', by a wealth tax, a gifts tax, the public ownership of land, and to communicate to the country a clear vision
of a fairer and more equal Britain.

There is nothing wrong with the Labour Party that a critical
self-examination cannot put right. There is no excuse for the
current defeatism in some sections of the party. It is astonishing

that after the experience of June 1970, not to mention the innumerable electoral upsets in every democratic country in the world, any experienced politician should write off an election in advance: still more astonishing for any Labour politician capable of reading the current economic forecasts.

If the deficiencies I have described are remedied, as they will be, then I for one shall face the next election with robust and cheerful optimism.

Part Two

Housing

6 *National Objectives in Housing*

Extract from Fabian Tract 410 Towards a Labour Housing Policy, *published in September 1971. The Fabian pamphlet was based on the Herbert Morrison Memorial Lecture delivered to an audience of Labour Party members in the Greater London area in July 1971.*

In this lecture I think aloud about housing policy—about the principles on which it should be based, what went right and what went wrong from 1964 to 1970, and how we could do better next time.

I start with the record. The Labour Government built more houses than ever before in a similar period; 25 per cent more in 1964–70 than the Conservatives built in the preceding six years, or five houses built under Labour for every four built under the Conservatives.

We greatly increased the subsidies paid to local authorities, and so helped to keep council rents at reasonable levels at a time of exceptionally high interest rates And when Tory Councils threatened unreasonable rent increases, we took legislative action through the 1969 Rent (Control of Increases) Act to moderate them.

We gave much increased help to owner-occupiers and enabled lower-income families to join their ranks through the option mortgage scheme and the provision of 100 per cent mortgages. In 1970, for the first time—and under a Labour Government—more than half the householders in England and Wales were owner-occupiers.

We gave fresh impetus to the improvement of older houses. Massive new help was provided under the 1969 Act, and 1970 saw a steep rise in the number of improvement grants taken up—a trend which is continuing.

We put an end to a hundred years of injustice by leasehold reform, and brought security of tenure and fair rents to private tenants under the 1965 Rent Act.

All these were solid advances; and they added up to a more comprehensive housing policy than has ever existed before in this country. But while we can take a proper pride in this achievement, the brutal fact remains that we did not solve the housing problem, which had for so long been underestimated; and well before June 1970 it had become abundantly clear that major changes were needed in our housing policies.

The sharp drop in house building after the peak year of 1968—partly, but not wholly, due to a deliberate go-slow by Conservative authorities—was a deeply disturbing development. In London especially, homelessness, overcrowding and insecurity were actually increasing. Slum clearance was proceeding much too slowly. Although the amount and scope of Government financial aid greatly increased, it was not related in any consistent way either to need or to equity. It did not reach down to the poorest families, who remained largely dependant on the Supplementary Benefits Commission (S.B.C.). Council-house rents were in a muddle, with wildly varying policies being pursued in different parts of the country. No help was given to private tenants—except for those whose rent was paid by the S.B.C.—even though they constitute the poorest group of householders; and furnished accommodation remained outside the Rent Acts, despite growing evidence of abuses in this sector. Meanwhile the best-off group, the owner-occupiers, received an open-ended subsidy.

So even had we won the Election, we should have wanted a radical re-examination of our policies. Indeed, such an examination was already far advanced within the Ministry of Housing, even before the election campaign began. On what principles should a revised Labour housing policy be based? I believe there is no one single principle, for housing policy has multiple objectives. We have a *social service* objective; that housing policy should play its part in the relief of poverty. We have a *housing* objective; to provide an adequate total stock of housing, of the kind that people want, where they want, and at prices which they can afford. We have a *planning* and *environmental* objective; housing policy must fit in with regional land-use plans, and must contribute to the improvement of the total environment. We have an *equity* objective; that the pattern of housing finance should be fair, as between different categories, and consistent with our total view of the right distribution of income. And we have an *economic* objective; to maintain the construction industry at a stable size, adequate to meet the demands of the years ahead.

I start with the basic question: how many houses do we need to build in order to attain these objectives? This is an extremely difficult question to answer. Since there is not, and cannot be, a free market in housing, we have no exact means of measuring potential *demand*. Surprisingly little is known about people's *aspirations* for different types and standards of housing. And any definition of *need* depends heavily on subjective judgments.

The underlying position is well known. There is a statistical surplus of dwellings over households—in 1970, 18·6 million dwellings, 18·3 million households. The occupancy rate is amongst the lowest in the world. The housing stock is comparatively good by Western European standards, and the birthrate is exceptionally low. Yet there is still a serious, and in some parts of the country desperate, housing problem. How is this so?

Firstly, this global statistical surplus conceals sharp regional variations and local imbalances. In some areas, notably London, there is a problem of homelessness which, as the Greve Report has shown, is actually growing worse year by year. And while overcrowding, in the old Victorian sense of very high room densities and grossly insanitary conditions, has largely disappeared as a national problem, there is still a great deal of involuntary sharing. The Greve Report shows that 1·4 million people, in Greater London alone, are living in shared accommodation; and particularly in the inner Boroughs, the proportion of people sharing or living insecurely in furnished rooms is rising. So there is here a serious current shortage, notably in respect of households now sharing, who clearly want a home of their own.

Secondly, there will be a heavy future need for more housing as a result of new household formation. Although the population of the United Kingdom is rising slowly by international standards, and indeed a good deal more slowly than was forecast even a few years ago, it is still expected to rise by 10·4 millions between now and the end of the century. The number of households also depends on wider social and economic factors. There is a strong tendency for households, other than families, to be formed—one, instead of two-person households, formed by elderly people, unmarried men and women, the widowed, the divorced, and young adults, including growing numbers of students. This tendency for people to set up on their own—in the jargon, this growth in 'headship rates'—will probably become still more marked with rising living standards and changing social patterns, notably amongst the elderly and the young. At the present time there is no adequate provision for it; in particular, there is not nearly enough provision for small dwellings. Just as the global surplus conceals shortages in particular areas, so it conceals shortages for particular categories.

Thirdly, in a mobile, industrialized society there is a need for a reasonable margin of vacant houses. The present vacancy rate is 2 per cent which is too low. It is probably necessary to have a vacancy reserve of at least 5 per cent, to encourage mobility, plus a further 1 per cent to meet the growing demand for second homes.

Fourthly, much of the present housing stock is not fit for human habitation, by the standards of the 1970s. There are still slums which are a national disgrace in this day and age. There are some four million dwellings, nearly a quarter of the housing stock, which are either officially unfit or lack one or other of the basic amenities. And to that, one must add the process of annual obsolescence, remembering that a third of the housing stock was built before the First World War.

By common consent, this backlog of sub-standard housing is being cleared much too slowly. Yet it is not easy to set an exact annual target for replacement since there are several variables here. One, obviously, is the priority one gives to clearing obsolescence, as compared with other social objectives —does one aim to replace all unfit dwellings in ten, fifteen or twenty years? Another priority is that rehabilitation is often an alternative to replacement. For myself, I think we have had too much of the bulldozer, and have destroyed too many old houses and whole communities with them; the 1969 Act, with its new emphasis on improvement, will in my view, prove one of the lasting achievements of the Labour Government. Yet there is still strong disagreement about how much weight should be placed on improvement as opposed to replacement.

But the biggest complication is that obsolescence is not merely a physical concept; there is now the problem of 'social obsolescence'. As living standards rise, the definition of what is sub-standard begins to go far beyond the purely structural and therefore measurable deficiencies of the house itself—it extends to the whole environment. Professor Colin Buchanan, in his report for the Nationwide Building Society,[1] has argued that people will increasingly want a middle-class standard of housing; and this he defines in terms of greater privacy, larger houses, and more private space around the house for the car, children's play, gardening, hobbies, sitting out of doors, and generally mucking about. This would mean detached houses at much lower than present densities, and would imply a positively gigantic programme of replacement.

Now I do not know whether Professor Buchanan is right. Perhaps he is, in which case the dominant pattern of the future will be the 'garden city' or the Surrey stockbroker belt. But perhaps he is not; many people may still prefer the traditional semi-detached, if it is cheaper; still more may prefer an urban pattern, or living in rehabilitated terrace housing, or in low blocks of flats; after all, lots of middle-class people like living in Chelsea. In Scandinavia most new building consists of apartments; even in the United States, with all its ample space, 45 per cent of all new housing is in apartments.

I do not know the answer. I mention the point only to demonstrate that there is no unique and objective way of setting a total housing target. We can easily set a minimum figure which will meet the most pressing and urgent needs. But above that minimum, the target will depend on a set of personal and social judgments; in particular, over how many years do we seek to replace or improve the existing stock of obsolescent dwellings, and how do we define obsolescence in the future, when we take account of these wider environmental factors? It is this which explains the huge variation in the housing targets set by different experts—from Professor Parry Lewis's 300,000 a year to Professor Colin Buchanan's 500,000.

However, what is obvious is that the country cannot possibly afford the present *drop* in housing output. Homelessness and sharing are on the increase, especially in London. Slum clearance is proceeding far too slowly. The needs of new types of smaller households are not being met. There are acres of dreary sub-standard housing in the intermediate and development areas of the Midlands and the North. And while the general stock is tolerable, by international standards, it is getting rapidly older; and the stock of new buildings is growing very slowly. So, while we cannot set an exact target for a future Labour Government in three to four years' time, we can clearly state that the present loss of momentum and urgency is intolerable and that we need an intensified effort for at least a decade ahead if we are to break the back of the quantitative problem.

This view is confirmed by international comparisons

(though one should treat these cautiously, inasmuch as the British figures take less credit for improvement than other countries' figures). In 1968, residential construction as a percentage of G.N.P. was as follows: France 6·7 per cent, Japan 6.5 per cent, Sweden 6·2 per cent, Germany 5 per cent, the United States 3·6 per cent, United Kingdom 3·7 per cent. Similarly, E.E.C. figures for dwellings completed per 100 of population show a lower figure for Britain than for France, Germany or Holland. These comparisons seem to support the case for our devoting a higher proportion of G.N.P. to housing and raising our output substantially above the depressed levels of the last three years.

But why should it be the responsibility of government to ensure that these various needs are met? Why do we not leave the provision of housing, as we do the provision of motor cars, to market forces and the play of supply and demand?

The reason is that housing is basic to certain socialist objectives. Firstly, homelessness, overcrowding and slums are a crucial facet of the poverty and squalor which it is Labour's first objective to eliminate. It is in this respect that we regard housing as a welfare or social service.

Secondly, we have a wider ideal of social equality, which requires (I quote from my Fabian pamphlet *A Social-Democratic Britain*)[2] 'an improvement in our social capital such that the less well-off have access to housing, health and education of a standard comparable, at least in the basic decencies, to that which the better-off can buy for themselves out of their private means.' In the case of housing, this access need not be completely free. We do not make the same paternalistic judgment which we make in respect of education; people demand, and must have some choice about, how much housing of what sort they want. But it must be possible—indeed, it is in our view a basic right of citizenship—for every household, especially families with young children, but also the growing numbers of young married couples and pensioners, to have a minimum civilized standard of dwelling, adequate for a decent, comfortable and private household life.

Thirdly, since housing is an element in the total environment, it concerns not merely the individual but society at large. Its location is a key factor in regional planning; its layout and design will determine whether our cities are hideous or tolerable, what our countryside looks like, and generally our national standards of space, architecture and amenity.

These objectives will not be met by the free play of market forces (if indeed one could ever imagine such a thing in housing). A free market is wholly irrelevant to the most urgent problem, since the homeless and over-crowded are generally poor people, who could not conceivably afford the market price of decent housing. Similarly with slum clearance and replacement, working-class families could not afford rents which would cover the economic cost of acquiring, demolishing and rebuilding whole areas of sub-standard housing. And even with rising incomes, a free market and free consumer choice would not meet the environmental needs; too little would be spent on improvement, too little on new housing with higher standards of space and amenity.

So one cannot have a market solution to the housing problem. Some part of the building programme must be public; some part of the housing stock must be leased or owned at less than the economic cost; and the government must bear a final responsibility for the overall housing situation.

What then do we need to achieve our objectives? We certainly need radical changes in current policies for the reasons I gave earlier. What form these should take are discussed in the remaining five contributions to Part Two of this volume.

7 Twelve Points for a Labour Housing Policy

Originally published in the Guardian *on December 15th, 1971.*

As the Labour Party begins the task of formulating new policies, I offer the following twelve points as the basis for a future Labour housing policy.

The hard core of the housing problem now lies in the stress areas of our large cities. This is where the slums, the homelessness and the overcrowding are concentrated; and so far from getting better, the position is if anything deteriorating, especially in London. The first objective of housing policy, is therefore, to reverse the recent disastrous decline in urban house-building. This will depend on money, machinery and political will.

1. Subsidies must be redistributed towards the urban areas of greatest need. This the Government claim to be achieving by their new proposals. But we have found, by persistent questioning in committee, that the claim is false. Few areas will gain from the alleged redistribution after the first few years; none will gain sufficiently.

For the Government are essentially engaged on a money-saving exercise; and the total cut in subsidies is far too severe to permit any effective redistribution. But Labour, while opposing the total cut, should accept the case for a restructuring of subsidies in the interests of the worst-off areas.

2. Even if they have the money, the inner-city areas lack the land they need for building houses. They cannot solve their housing problems within their own boundaries; they must have the help of the suburbs, overspill and New Towns. This

calls for a metropolitan strategy and a machinery for implementing that strategy. Neither exist at the moment, nor will they under the Government's proposals for local government reform. Labour must therefore examine the case for joint Metropolitan Housing Agencies for London and the other major conurbations.

3. But the political will may still be lacking. Conservative councils, as we have seen since 1968, may simply decline to build whatever the need. A future Labour Government must therefore have stronger default powers than in the past. Mr Peter Walker has now taken Draconian reserve powers, including the power to send in a Whitehall Housing Commissioner, to compel reluctant councils to comply with his 'fair rent' proposals. We must formulate comparable default powers to deal with councils which refuse to build.

4. The private rented sector is likely to continue its slow decline. But providing, as it does, much of the cheap rented housing in the worst stress areas, it remains of great importance; and its decline carries the danger that badly needed low-income housing will disappear into middle-class owner-occupation.

This danger must be met, partly by a more systematic policy of municipalization, partly by greater help for those housing associations which specialize in rehabilitating cheap rented property, and partly by repealing the many open invitations in the Housing Finance Bill to exploitation and harassment by the remaining private landlords.

5. The trend to owner-occupation, supported as it is by both political parties, will continue—unless, as currently seems possible, an uncontrollable rise in land prices puts home-ownership out of the reach even of better-off wage-earners. The country now has no land policy save exhortation; and exhortation never defeated market forces.

Labour must urgently seek a solution to this problem, and in this search it may well have to go radically further than its two previous attempts at a solution—the Land Commission and the 1947 Act.

The Conservative proposals for so-called 'fair' council-house rents have at least made us think harder about the principles on which public sector rents should be based. Clear principles emerge from the current debate.

6. Rents must be set at a level which the majority of tenants can pay without rebate. For if, as the Government now propose, they are set at a level so high that most tenants (including many earning £40 a week) are eligible for rebate, means-testing will be introduced on a hitherto unprecedented scale. An army of bureaucrats will be employed to pay back part of the excessive rent in rebates. There is the risk of a low take-up of rebates with consequent family hardship. And the creation of yet another means-tested benefit aggravates the increasingly serious problem of working-class incentives.

7. Council rents should bear some relation to cost. The Government, on the contrary, are proposing a level of rents, which over much of the country, will produce a profit in the housing revenue account; and half the profit will go to the Exchequer. Many council tenants will thus pay, on top of their ordinary rates and taxes, an additional tax or levy through their rents. This is wholly wrong. Council tenants in any local authority area should not pay a total rent-income which exceeds the historic costs of providing the housing in which they live.

8. Rent policy cannot be divorced from prices and incomes policy as a whole. Rents are a particularly sensitive aspect of the cost of living, and their behaviour has a powerful influence on wage-claims and cost-inflation. You cannot, as the Government propose, force up the rents of some millions of tenants by up to 25 per cent a year—and then expect the unions to moderate their wage-claims.

I do not mean that we should irresponsibly promise great reductions in rent or miraculously costless housing. But a Labour policy for rents must be consistent with our anti-inflationary strategy as a whole (when we get one).

9. The concept of a national rent-rebate scheme for those

with low incomes is in my view right (though the numbers affected would be vastly lower under the above principles than under 'fair' or market rents).

The new rent allowance for the private tenant is also to be welcomed. But the cost of these rebates and allowances should fall on the State and not, as the Government propose, in large part on other council tenants and local ratepayers. The relief of poverty is a national, not a local, responsibility; and its cost should be borne by central government and the national tax-payer.

10. One group conspicuously gains no help from the new proposals—the furnished tenants. They number only some half a million households. But they have the lowest incomes of any section of the community; they pay the highest price per room; and they have the least security. Following the Francis Report, they are to remain deprived of full Rent Act protection; and under the new Housing Bill they are excluded from the private rent allowance. A Labour housing policy would reverse both these decisions.

11. There is one thing which does not figure prominently, in the current fashionable talk about participation, but which in truth cries out for more democracy and participation—the management of council estates.

At present, the role of the council is that of the traditional landlord. It can evict a tenant almost at will, as certain recent well-publicized cases have shown. It decides, usually without consultation, what play facilities will or will not be provided, what repairs will or will not be done, what pets may or may not be kept. And there is no right of appeal against its decisions.

It is these aspects of traditional landlordism, and not just the financial advantages of the owner-occupier, which often make the council tenant seem, both to himself and to others, to be a second-class citizen. We must seek to give him a security, an independence and a freedom to do what he likes in his home, which is comparable with that of the owner-occupier.

A programme for greater tenants' democracy should therefore form a central, and probably the most novel, part of a Labour housing policy. It must include specific and definite rights; to be granted security of tenure; to improve the house in which he lives; to participate in managing the estate on which he lives; to be represented on the relevant council committee; and generally to be consulted on any decision which directly affects his home and his environment.

Mr Dick Leonard's Bill points the way. Miss Della Nevitt has outlined important proposals in her *Fair Deal for House-holders*.[1] We must now add to these a systematic set of proposals to introduce a proper equality of status as between tenant and home-owner.

12. A Labour housing policy should be imbued with a philosophy of free choice. It must wholly reject the Tory philosophy, enshrined in the present Housing Bill, that some people 'should' be council tenants and others owner-occupiers, that council houses are only for certain categories of person and not for others.

It is this philosophy which creates the feeling of first and second-class citizens, and would relegate public housing to being a one-class welfare service. Labour's objective, by contrast, should be to equalize the status and financial advantages of different types of occupancy, and then let people choose freely between them.

Much detail now needs to be added to these twelve points. But they constitute the essential check-list against which any future Labour housing policy must be measured.

8 *Housing and Equality*

Originally published in the Guardian *on June 15th, 1971.*

It is a great comfort that everyone now seems to agree that socialism is about equality. The Fabian critique of the Labour Government's social record is entitled *Labour and Inequality*.[1] Wilfred Beckerman, in introducing *The Labour Government's Economic Record 1964–70*,[2] writes of 'the prime importance of the equality objective in differentiating the Labour Party from the Conservative Party.' A recent international seminar which I attended in Japan confirmed that this was the standpoint of most social-democratic parties in the developed world.

Tawney would have rejoiced at all this; and so do I. But while this rediscovery of equality is exceedingly welcome, it has certain implications which are not always faced. First, it will not carry conviction if it takes the form of purely negative criticism of the past, or mere declaratory statements of intent about the future.

For if we are such ardent egalitarians now, why did we not do more when we had the chance? If we now say that we must abolish poverty, have a tax on wealth, spend more on housing and education, do more for the regions, step up overseas aid— who or what stopped us from achieving these admirable aims between 1964 and 1970? In the light of past failures, declaratory platitudes will not be enough; the sceptical voters will want to see the colour of our money—and that means *policies* which are evidently practical and realistic. Otherwise a yawning credibility gap will open up.

The voters will be even more sceptical if these ringing declarations go hand in hand with an adherence, or even only an obeisance, to the currently fashionable doctrine of anti-growth. It is no good telling them that another 2 per cent of G.N.P. is to be spent on education, and an extra 1 per cent on housing, and an additional 1 per cent on abolishing poverty; that we shall simultaneously spend more on curing pollution and improving the environment; that we also wish our working-class constituents to enjoy a middle-class standard of life, which is what they rightly want; and finally that we shall be far more generous to the developing countries—all out of a 2 per cent annual rate of growth.

Of course the voters, being sensible people, won't believe it. This is not Japan, with a 10 per cent growth-rate. The United Kingdom is the slowest-growing country in the world. If anyone thinks that we should slow down the country's growth-rate still further, they had better be chary of declaratory promises.

With these warnings in mind, and following on my *Guardian* article of last December, I turn to the question of equality in housing.

The essential requirement, obviously, is to reduce the gross inequality in *physical* housing conditions; and that means first and foremost providing everyone with a home of a civilized minimum standard of quality, comfort and privacy.

To achieve this, housing investment will need to be lifted far above the present abysmally low level. This does not mean adopting another grandiose target of 500,000 new houses a year—partly because housing must be judged against other competing claims on limited resources, but also because improvement is often an alternative to new housing.

Population is increasing at only a minimal rate; and home-lessness and overcrowding, though desperate where they exist, are mainly to be found in the centres of large cities. Over much of the country the problem is rather one of slums and *unfit* housing—of the disgraceful number of houses without a bath, hot water or inside lavatory.

But here we have an element of choice. We can either

demolish, clear and redevelop, or we can improve and re-habilitate. A huge target for *new* houses implies a decision in favour of clearance and against rehabilitation—at a time when opinion is moving strongly towards the latter. The sensible target nationally is one which embraces both new housing and improvement; the sensible objective locally is to *renew* entire areas of bad housing by a mixture of different methods.

Housing investment, thus defined, must be substantially raised. It must also be redistributed, with a greater emphasis on the inner urban stress areas where the homelessness and over-crowding are concentrated, and on council building, now at an appallingly low level, since those below the minimum standard will not find decent housing in the private market.

This redistribution requires a reorganization of building subsidies, new regional or metropolitan building agencies, and an attitude to council housing diametrically opposed to that of Mr Peter Walker.

But above all it requires a reform of housing finance. People in bad housing normally cannot *afford* good housing. It is no good investing more in housing for the poor unless we enable them to pay for it. And if our object is not simply to eliminate the worst housing, but more generally to reduce inequality, then the present distribution of financial aid is strikingly perverse.

The biggest share goes to owner-occupiers, and takes the form of mortage interest tax-relief. This now costs the Ex-chequer £300 millions per annum (or £60 per mortgaged house) and is rising rapidly.

It is clearly a subsidy, since it reduces the cost of buying a house below the economic price. And it is highly inegalitarian in its effects. It brings no help to those on the lowest incomes, who cannot afford to buy in any case; generally, it goes to a group which is better-off, on average, than either council or private tenants; and within this group it gives the most relief to those on the highest incomes. The option mortgage scheme has slightly improved matters at the bottom end of the scale, but aid to the owner-occupier remains extremely regressive.

Subsidies to council housing amount to £157 millions, plus £60 millions from the rates, making £39 per council dwelling. This aid goes to a group with generally lower incomes than owner-occupiers. But not only is it smaller in total; it is also haphazardly distributed. For being paid out under several different Housing Acts, it goes to local authorities, not according to housing needs or income levels, but to the historical accident of when they built up their housing stock.

The lowest incomes, as well as the worst housing, exist in the private rented sector. Yet this sector received no financial aid until the introduction of the private rent allowance; and even that does not yet extend to furnished tenants, who have the lowest incomes of all.

Improvement grants, although highly successful in improving the housing stock, also operate regressively. They are overwhelmingly taken up by better-off owner-occupiers and speculative property developers, who receive not only the amount of the grant, but also an appreciation in the capital value of the house.

The only Government payments which go unequivocally to those in need are the rent allowances of the Supplementary Benefits Commission; and these can scarcely be classed as housing aid.

Direct financial aid is not the whole story; there are other ways in which different housing groups gain relatively more or less. The owner-occupier, now relieved of Schedule A, pays no tax on his imputed rent income. But the tenant pays his rent out of income which has been fully taxed, while the private landlord pays Schedule D on his rent income in the same way as any other investor. This exemption from tax, of rent income in kind, is worth more to the owner-occupier than mortgage tax-relief; the Fabian authors reckon its value at some £700 millions a year.

Unlike the tenant, the owner-occupier gains from inflation;

he repays his mortgage in depreciated pounds. Since, moreover, house prices rise faster than prices generally, he has a profitable investment on which he makes a real capital gain; and, unlike the private landlord, he pays no tax on that gain.

And so on and so on; the complexities are endless. But the broad picture is clear. Taking both open and hidden subsidies together, the pattern of housing aid is inequitable and regressive. And, as I explained at length during its committee stage, the Housing Finance Bill will make matters worse.

Four things are needed in order to lessen inequality. Firstly, more help must be given to those on lower incomes, through a national system of rebates and allowances. But this must be financed out of general taxation and not, as the Tories propose, largely from the rents of better-off council tenants.

Secondly, while the method of aid to home-buyers should be maintained, the total must be redistributed. More help should be given to those who cannot now afford a mortgage; and this should be paid for by restricting the relief given to surtax payers.

Thirdly, subsidies to the council sector must, contrary to what the Tories propose, be kept broadly equal to the aid given to the owner-occupied sector; while rent policy should be based on the principles described in my previous *Guardian* article.

But, lastly, none of this will be sufficient without a policy for house prices, which means a policy for the public ownership of building land. For the present manic rise in prices fosters speculative investment demand for houses, which distorts the choice between buying and renting. And it creates a hideous two-nation pattern of housing, both through the middle-class takeover of previously working-class areas and by pricing house-purchase far out of the reach of even the relatively prosperous working class.

9 A New Deal for Council Tenants

Originally published in the Guardian *on June 16th, 1971.*

Equality in housing, as in other fields, is mainly a matter of finance, but not wholly so. Whether people feel, and appear to others, privileged or under-privileged, equal or superior or inferior, depends also on a host of non-financial factors. And judged in this wider sense of social status, the council tenant and the owner-occupier are by no means equal

There is still, though less than in the past, a taint attached to living in a council house—a whiff of the welfare, of subsidization, of huge uniform estates, and generally of second-class citizenship.

Now some of this prejudice is based on objective fact; the council tenant *is* an under-privileged citizen, in important respects which I discuss later. But much of it stems from a pervasive feeling, insidiously fostered by the present Government, that council housing is *meant* only for poorer people; better-off people should, as a matter of course, move out and invest in a house of their own. Home-ownership is praised as not only financially advantageous (which Heaven knows it is), but morally laudable, bringing out sturdy British virtues of self-help and independence. Renting, by contrast, is undignified, fit for poorer people, but reprehensible for anyone owning colour television or a (mythical) Jaguar. These feelings are, of course, intensified by the myth that all council tenants are subsidized, whereas owner-occupiers are not.

For myself, I reject the view that municipal housing should

be purely a welfare service or safety-net for people who cannot be housed by the private sector. I believe it must be the main provider of housing for all those who wish to rent. I believe this, not only on principle, but for a severely practical reason.

The dominant feature of the housing scene has long been, and still is, the decline of the private rented sector. In 1914, 90 per cent of homes were rented from private landlords. By 1950 this had fallen to 45 per cent, by 1960 to 26 per cent and last year to 14 per cent. There is no likelihood that the trend will be reversed.

I welcome this decline—though not, as I shall show, its short-term consequences. Private landlordism is not an appropriate form of house-ownership in an advanced society. The relationship between landlord and tenant is too unequal; and the landlord wields a degree of power over his tenant's life which is unacceptable in a democratic society. This is especially so when, as today, economic circumstances combine to give the landlord an overwhelming financial incentive to get rid of poor tenants and sell or lease to richer ones; and when, as is generally the case in the urban stress areas, the tenants are those with the lowest incomes, the least bargaining power and the worst prospects of finding alternative accommodation.

One may pass all the laws in the world against harassment and eviction, but the contest is too unequal, and the inevitable result is the insecurity and bitterness seen today in Islington or North Kensington.

Middle-class tenants are now feeling the same pressures. As renting becomes less and less profitable, compared with selling, speculators and property companies buy up blocks of flats over the heads of the tenants, who first learn the news when they face a doubling of rents or service charge or, most commonly, a demand either to buy or quit. The insecurity is now intolerable; no wonder middle-class tenants are in revolt, anathematizing Freshwater or First National Finance as violently as any working-class militants.

The private landlord, then, is getting out; and a good thing too. But in the process, unfortunately, a lot of rented accommodation is disappearing into owner-occupation. This accommodation, especially in the cities, is desperately badly needed. It provides a large part of the cheap housing available to low-income families; generally it provides for all those groups who need to rent.

For large blocks of flats, the answer will often lie in co-operative ownership. But the main responsibility must fall on local authorities, both to give maximum encouragement to housing associations, which specialize in rehabilitating older rented property, and more directly to undertake a planned and systematic policy of municipalization. The powers of compulsory purchase must now be vigorously used, to take over and preserve badly-needed rented housing.

In the process, local authorities will become the main provider of unfurnished rented housing; and the notion that council housing is a welfare service, only for those who cannot *afford* to buy, will seem more and more wrong-headed. For people from a variety of occupations, backgrounds, income-levels and ages will always positively *prefer* renting to buying—elderly people too old to take out a mortgage, unmarried professional workers, widowed or divorced people, mobile workers, students, and so on. Local authorities must now take responsibility for meeting the total demand for rented accommodation from whatever source it comes.

This change in itself will raise the status of council housing. But positive improvements are also needed.

Firstly, *more choice*: not only is council housing too standardized in size, offering inadequate choice, both to very large and very small households, but its design is imposed from above, with little effort to discover how people actually *want* to live. One year the architects and planners are mad for comprehensive redevelopment and tower blocks; the next year, they are equally mad for rehabilitation and low-rise.

In neither case do they ask the prospective tenants; they only guess at how their preferences divide between a house with a garden, a high-rise flat and rehabilitated terrace housing. Yet Oldham has shown from the top, and Golborne from the bottom, that things can be done more democratically; and they must be done so in future.

Secondly, *more community services*: council estates, particularly tower blocks, often exist for years without adequate shops, pubs, play areas, a community centre, a library or a youth club. It is somehow assumed that council tenants want only a roof over their head and have no other social needs.

Thirdly, *more variety*: council estates, particularly outside the cramped centres of large cities, are not usually the vast, uniform, soulless and segregated places which middle-class critics seem to imagine; they are normally well liked and well laid out.

Nevertheless, we should seek a greater variety and inter-mingling, with smaller estates, more general improvement areas, the insertion of new housing in town centres, and so on. Different types of tenure should always be mixed, with council and private housing juxtaposed; this will happen more easily if, as I hope, councils both take over private rented property and themselves begin to build for sale (a much better policy than the indiscriminate sale of existing council houses).

And we should strongly encourage the 'third arm' of housing associations and co-operatives; we do not want all housing to be either municipal or individually owned. The object should be the maximum degree of choice, muddle and variety.

Fourthly, *more security*: at present, a council can evict a tenant on a magistrate's court order at four weeks' notice; it is not even obliged to give its reasons. True, in spite of some frightening individual cases, councils do not generally abuse their power, but good administration is not a substitute for individual rights. The council tenant should be given the same security and right of appeal as the private tenant has under the 1968 Rent Act. And we could extend security of tenure still further, by giving long-term agreements.

Lastly, *more democracy*: a council's relationship with its tenants is still that of the traditional landlord. It decides what repairs are to be done, what pets may be kept, what colour the doors will be painted, what play areas there should be, where a fence should be put up, what services should be provided in what order. The tenant is not consulted; and he has no right of appeal. He has far less freedom than the owner-occupier to do what he likes in and around his home; and this is a major cause of his inferior status.

A few councils, notably in London, have accepted the argument and set up machinery, based broadly on Mr Dick Leonard's Private Member's Bill, for tenants' participation in management decisions. Elected tenants' representatives sit on joint-area housing committees and on the relevant subcommittee of the council itself; and the area committees decide their own priorities from lists of possible estate improvements.

As a result, the council makes more acceptable decisions; and the tenants, while learning that choices have to be made, help to determine what those choices are and in consequence feel better treated.

The logical conclusion of this approach would be full tenants' management or even co-operative ownership of council estates. These possibilities are currently being examined in an important study commissioned by Lambeth Borough Council. I hope this will lead to a diversity of experiment with different forms of co-operative management.

The object of all these changes, financial and otherwise, is simple. It is to equalize the status and financial advantages of different types of housing tenure, both for the sake of greater equality and to give more choice and variety.

10 *The Case for Municipalization*

Originally published in the Guardian *on November 2nd, 1972.*

The privately rented sector of housing has three obvious characteristics. Firstly, it provides the worst standard of housing of any sector, containing 14 per cent of all dwellings but 50 per cent of unfit dwellings.

Secondly, it is disproportionately concentrated in the areas of housing stress, accounting (for example) for well over half the housing in most of the deprived areas recently analysed by Shelter.[1] Generally, its tenants have the lowest incomes of any housing group.

Thirdly, no post-war Government has produced a policy which combines a reasonable protection for the tenant with a commercial profit for the landlord; so the sector has been the scene of continuous tension and dispute. Particularly under Tory Governments, the attempt to make it profitable has created a succession of appalling social upheavals from Rachmanism under Mr Henry Brooke, to the present crisis under Mr Peter Walker.

This, then, is the problem sector of British housing. But need we worry too much about it now? It has, after all, been in continuous decline since the First World War, 90 per cent of dwellings in 1914, 45 per cent in 1950, 14 per cent today; and the decline is certain to continue. The financial and tax advantages of selling, rather than letting, residential property are overwhelming. So the existing landlord continues to get out, pocketing his improvement grant on the way; and new investment goes elsewhere. Not even the sops in the Housing

Finance Act—the decontrol and the higher rents—will reverse the process.

So why not let private landlordism die a natural death, merely giving some badly needed pain-killing injections in the meantime, protection for the furnished tenant, stiffer penalties for harassment and so on?

The answer is clear. The numbers involved are too great, over 2½ million households, and the death-throes too violent.

I am not, at the best of times, a natural friend of the commercial landlord. But at the worst of times, that is, in the areas of housing stress, with which this article is mainly concerned, he wields, and continually abuses, a wholly unacceptable power over other individuals. In spite of all the protection given by Labour Governments since 1945, tenants live in constant insecurity, often not knowing who their landlord is, uneasily aware that their homes are being bought and sold above their heads, certain only of two things: the huge speculative profits being made at their expense, and the relentless pressure on them to pay up or get out. This is now as true of middle-class tenants of the Freshwater group as of the poor, often black, often uneducated under-class of Notting Hill.

There is not only the immediate human misery; equally serious is the long-term loss of low-income rented housing, as developers force out existing tenants and sell their properties to richer clients. The country cannot afford this loss—least of all when *public* building for rent (as measured by council house starts) is, under a Tory Government, at its lowest level for a decade. Housing associations struggle gallantly to stem the tide, but are often helpless in the face of currently inflated prices. What is needed is a large-scale transfer of the ownership of private rented property; and only the local authorities have the power, resources and experience to achieve it.

Municipalization would bring other advantages in its train. Acquiring as they would a more diverse housing stock, local authorities could offer *all* tenants a wider choice of accommodation—not just a home on a purpose-built council estate, but a variety of sizes, shapes, ages and locations. Thus a more advantageous use could be made of the existing stock.

I have long thought that in the post-war world too much has been demolished and too little improved. Not only is improvement less costly than comprehensive redevelopment, so that it gives good housing at less expense; it also avoids the break-up of communities, and it preserves a social and architectural scale which people increasingly cherish. Often, of course, councils have no alternative but to use the bulldozer. Nevertheless, as they themselves take over much of the remaining unfit housing, they will be able, and indeed compelled, to make a more conscious and considered choice between demolition and improvement.

What are the practical issues involved? Since the urgency of the problem varies from place to place, being infinitely more pressing in Islington than in Grimsby, central government should not lay down a uniform national timetable; the attempt to do so was the weakness of Labour proposals in the 1950s. The pace should be a matter for local decision, subject only to strong government reserve powers.

Some Labour councils have already acquired substantial blocks of rented property by agreement. Where compulsion is needed, the necessary powers already exist under Sections 96-7 of the 1957 Housing Act; and the next Labour Government should, immediately on its election, issue a circular stating that it would allow all compulsory purchase orders made under this Act on privately rented property. It could also, if necessary, introduce 'sale notices', compelling any landlord, wishing to sell rented accommodation to notify the council beforehand and give it first option to buy.

At present price levels, compensation would be exceedingly costly. The first priority is a policy for containing the price of housing; on this I hope to write later.

But whatever the cost, the investment will show a generous return. In the absence of municipalization, x number of rented houses will disappear into owner-occupation. If we wish to maintain—in fact, we must greatly increase—the pool of rented accommodation, then local authorities (if they have the land, which in the inner cities they may not) must build x additional new council houses to make good the loss. But it would be far cheaper to buy the original houses and renovate them. So municipalization will be an excellent bargain for tenant and taxpayer alike.

There is, therefore, a powerful case for a special municipalization subsidy. New council building, which should certainly attract large subsidies, adds some 2 per cent annually to the rented stock. But I am here talking of some 30 per cent of the rented stock. It is worth paying a lot to preserve this for desperately needed low-income housing.

Municipalization will at once symbolize and encourage the wider view now taken (except by Mr Walker and Mr Amery) of the role of local authorities in housing. It underlines the fact that they are responsible, not just for creating and managing council estates, but for the *total* housing situation in their area. And they are not in the business of rented accommodation solely to provide a welfare service for the poor; with the demise of the private landlord, they must meet the demand for renting from whatever source it comes.

But these wider responsibilities confer corresponding obligations. For example, it will be even more essential to raise local authority standards of maintenance. If newly municipalized property is as mismanaged as many G.L.C. estates today, municipalization will be a political catastrophe. People can only grumble at a private landlord; they can vote against a public one.

Low or (perhaps even more irritating) capricious standards of maintenance are a reflection of a deeper ill. Some councils adopt an autocratic attitude towards their tenants, such as would never be tolerated in modern industry.

I hope that councils will do voluntarily what is needed. But let us encourage them with some competition. While they will certainly be the main providers of rented accommodation in the future, they should not be the sole suppliers; monopoly is as undesirable in housing as it is elsewhere. It would give the council quite excessive power—where could an evicted tenant go? And it could not easily cater for all the varied needs of special groups—mobile workers, students, and the like.

Having municipalized, therefore, the council should often dispose of part of its newly acquired property. Some it might sell to sitting tenants for owner-occupation; and some it would, I hope, hand over to (recognized) housing associations; for we have here the opportunity to find a new and greatly expanded role for the voluntary housing movement.

We all pay lip-service to this movement, yet it never really gets off the ground; even now, it accounts for hardly 1 per cent of the housing stock. Labour councils have often been suspicious of it in the past, and not always without reason.

But the social and economic arguments for a flourishing 'third sector' override everything; and a policy for municipalization demands a concomitant policy for an ambitious expansion of the voluntary movement. This should allow a large place in particular for co-operative and co-ownership societies. To a co-operator like myself, these are eminently desirable in themselves; they are, however, the only long-term counter to the disruptive activities of Freshwater and First National Finance.

The private rented sector receives too little attention in the current housing debate. Even as it declines, it is the scene of the worst decay and exploitation; and the decline itself grievously threatens the balance of the housing stock. Municipalization is the only quick and practical answer. But having municipalized, we must then pursue our ultimate housing objective—the maximum degree of choice, variety and self-government.

11 *Housing: A Summing Up*

Originally published in the Guardian *on May 2nd and 3rd, 1973.*

The Conservative Government's housing policy, heralded in Fair Deal language as 'one of the great social reforms of the century', is now a shambles. Completions last year were the lowest for a decade. The cost of housing has soared at a rate never before experienced. The speculative profits from land have aroused universal revulsion. And public expenditure on housing has been redistributed away from the less well-off towards the better-off half of the population.

Does Labour have a coherent alternative policy? I have written on particular aspects of housing in previous *Guardian* articles. I seek now to draw the threads together.

The stock of housing in this country for the first time exceeds the number of potential households. At the same time, homelessness is increasing, and many, in desperate need, are unable to find a home. Why this apparent paradox?

Firstly, conditions vary enormously from one part of the country to another. In London there is a growing army of homeless, a crisis in the private rented sector and a mounting feeling of anger and despair. But in other regions, while many special needs remain unsatisfied, there is a marked improvement in the overall position; the condition of the stock is better, and empty properties are appearing on a growing scale. There is no longer a uniform national problem of quantitative shortage, but rather a series of diverse local problems.

Secondly, even *within* a particular locality the position is often complex. There are empty council houses, yet a still unsatisfied demand, both for owner-occupied houses and for particular types of council dwelling. The 'fit' is wrong; the available houses are not what people want; and people are now more choosy—they will not accept the first (or even the second or third) house offered them by the council. This is why, when I ask councillors in a town about their housing problem, I often get quite contradictory answers. Certainly no one in central Government is in a position to assess local needs in numerical terms.

Thirdly, in many regions the overriding problem now is one, not of shortage, but of unfit housing. Here there is often a choice between demolition and rehabilitation. For myself, I continue to think that too much has been, and is being, demolished, and in the process, consumer choice is being denied and the stock of cheap housing dangerously diminished.

Be that as it may, a choice exists; and it can only be made locally. A national target for new houses prejudges that choice; for it implies a certain rate of demolition and new building as opposed to rehabilitation.

I am therefore adamantly opposed to a *national* house-building target. It may have made sense in the earlier post-war years when the evident need was to build and build and build still more. It makes no sense in the far more diverse and complex conditions of today. The national housing programme should be the sum of a series of local decisions; and the function of government is to create the conditions in which local needs and demand can be met.

These conditions manifestly do not exist today. Both in the public and private sector, needs are being met too slowly. Yet, incredibly, the latest NEDO forecasts, predict a further *fall* in housebuilding in 1974-5. So, while one cannot lay down a precise national target, one can certainly make the broad judgment that total housing investment—including both rehabilitation and new building—should be substantially increased.

How? Firstly, the biggest constraint lies in the capacity of the construction industry, which is quite inadequate to meet a generally higher level of demand and especially local authority demand; councils cannot even get firms to tender in many parts of the country. The cause lies partly in the perennial crisis created by the 'lump', partly in the damaging effects of stop-go building society lending, partly in a chronic inefficiency. The cure must lie in legislating against the 'lump', controlling building society lending (to which I return later), and injecting some competitive public enterprise, through the expansion of direct labour departments (perhaps regionally organized) which would build for sale as well as for rent.

Secondly, finance—and especially local authority finance; for while it may be a desirable long-term aim to increase the ratio of owner-occupation, the immediate and urgent need is to provide more unfurnished rented accommodation, at reasonable prices, for those who cannot afford to buy. In the short term, the problem here is the cost yardstick. In the long term it is to direct adequate building subsidies to the urban areas of greatest stress. The Housing Finance Act purports to achieve this, but fails because the Government's determination to cut the *total* subsidy bill rules out any effective redistribution. A Labour Government would largely retain the new selective subsidies, but increase their *weighting* within the total of housing aid.

Thirdly, the supply of land—contrary to popular supposition and Ministerial statements, this is not the most serious constraint on the house-building programme: both the endless arguments about who is hoarding land, and the Government's land-hoarding charge and similar gimmicks, are relatively minor matters. The main exception is in some of the conurbations, and, above all, London. The Inner London Boroughs desperately lack land; and they must have access to land in the outer boroughs if they are to solve their housing problems. This, scandalously, the Tory-controlled outer boroughs refuse to provide, as Barnet has just rejected Brent. That is one (though not the only) reason why a succession of weighty reports—

Cullingworth,[1] Greve,[2] and now Layfield[3]—have rightly advocated a strategic Metropolitan Housing Authority.

What is needed is not only higher investment, but also the best use of the *existing* stock. This is not now achieved, partly because the distribution of population does not match the distribution of houses, partly because of the grossly passive attitude towards empty properties— 100,000 even in London— and often because local authority boundaries bear no relation to housing needs (which is why Layfield recommended a common waiting-list and basis of allocation for the whole of London).

But the crucial problem, the core of the urban housing problem, lies in the private rented sector. This is steadily shrinking as landlords find it far more profitable to improve and then sell their properties for owner-occupation. Even the Tory Government, in yet another astonishing ideological volte-face, has now conceded that the decline in private landlordism is unlikely to be reversed.

The only way of preserving this housing for the less well-off is to take it into municipal ownership. This suggestion still produces horror in the breasts of Tory Ministers and councillors. Yet it emerges steadily from a succession of authoritative reports, culminating in Layfield. Moreover the experiences of recent years—the speculative buying and selling of blocks of flats, the sudden increase in rent or service charges, the bullying, the insecurity—have converted many middle-class as well as working-class tenants to the Labour view that private landlordism is not an appropriate form of tenure in an advanced society.

Municipalization would not proceed at an equal gallop all over the country. In Kensington and Brent it is a top priority, and should form part of a co-ordinated metropolitan crash-programme to deal with every aspect of London's housing problem. But in Grimsby or Stoke-on-Trent, where the typical landlord owns only a house or two and 'gentrification' does not arise, it has a much lower priority. It is not necessary to have a uniform national timetable; the pace should be a matter for local decision, except in the inner urban stress areas, where Government reserve powers should, if necessary, be ruthlessly used to support the metropolitan crash-programme.

Municipalization does not mean that local authorities should become the sole providers of rented accommodation. Monopoly is as undesirable in housing as it is elsewhere. Having municipalized, the council should often dispose of its newly acquired property. Some it would sell to sitting tenants for owner-occupation; and some it would transfer to housing associations, cost-rent societies and tenants' co-operatives. I welcome the Government's new-found enthusiasm for the 'third sector' of the voluntary housing movement: we want the maximum degree of choice, variety and self-government in housing. I hope that the newly appointed Lord Goodman will pursue this objective; though I fear that he is mainly intended to stave off the horrors of municipalization.

In the very long run, the price of houses for sale rises broadly in line with incomes and the cost of construction. In the short run, however, the crucial determinant is the availability of credit. This depends overwhelmingly on the supply of building society lending, which depends in turn (since the societies traditionally lend virtually all that they borrow) on their inflow of funds.

This is a crazy system. On the borrowing side, building societies are in the highly competitive market for savings. Their inflow (especially as their borrowing rates tend to be sticky) fluctuates wildly with changes in competing interest rates and monetary conditions generally. These fluctuations, which have nothing whatever to do with the housing situation, are then communicated to the housing market.

Thus in both 1971 and 1972, when the societies were flush with funds, lending rose by over 30 per cent; but the supply of houses for sale rose by only 2½ per cent each year. The predictable result was an unprecedented explosion of house (and therefore land) prices, which fed on itself as speculative investment demand was superimposed on the normal demand for housing space. The rise in prices redistributed the limited supply of housing, away from the less well-off towards the better-off, and rewarded the existing owner at the expense of the new buyer.

Now the monetary conditions have gone into reverse and the societies are short of funds. So, although nothing has changed in the housing situation, there is a potential mortgage famine, a 9½ per cent lending rate, and the farce of the £15 million subsidy. And this grotesque instability deals yet another blow to the efficiency of the building industry.

The price and supply of housing are a central political issue; and control of mortgage lending, which so heavily influences them, can no longer be left to the building societies and market forces. The Government must now take the responsibility for matching the flow of funds to the pace of new building, whether by my proposed Stabilization Fund or some other means. There is also an overwhelming case, not (as some propose) for nationalizing the whole industry, but certainly for establishing a state-run society to provide a much-needed yardstick for costs and efficiency.

Council rents should be based on pooled historic costs; i.e. total rental income in each authority's area should be set to cover the costs of management, maintenance, and debt servicing (but not 'community' costs such as slum clearance).

No principle of rent-fixing is perfect, but pooled historic cost shows a clear balance of advantage over alternative bases for setting rents. It gives a rough equity with the owner-occupier whose mortgage repayments are based on historic cost. It is simple and widely understood.

The general level of pooled rents would not be unduly onerous as a proportion of earnings; fewer people would be forced to apply for a rebate; and rent rises would not have the disastrous effect which 'fair rents' have today on a prices and incomes policy. True, there would be quite wide variations from place to place; but these would often reflect genuine differences in economic circumstances, and in any case would diminish as rents were pooled over a wider area with local government reorganization. True, also, councils with a costly recent or current building programme would face special problems (as indeed they would under any system); and these would call for special subsidies.

While the private rented sector still exists, there is much to be said for the *principle* of the 1965 Act; for 'fair rents' here have a clear purpose which they lack in the council sector. But the *practice* is working out more harshly than the authors of that Act intended, due partly to wholesale Tory decontrol and partly to soaring market values. A limit should therefore be set to the annual increases permitted under the Act.

The price of land is of course relevant to all forms of housing, though it is house prices which have pushed up land prices and not, as is sometimes believed, the other way round. The Labour Party will shortly publish its detailed plans for taking development land into public ownership.

Government aid to housing is on a substantial scale. But its *distribution* makes for less equality, not more.

Much the biggest share goes to owner-occupiers in mortgage interest tax-relief. This is highly inegalitarian in its effects. It gives no help to those on the lowest incomes, who cannot afford to buy; it goes to a group which is better-off on average than either council or private tenants; within this group it gives the most relief to those on the highest incomes; and this is to say nothing of the additional advantages accruing to the owner-occupier from inflation, improvement grants, the absence of Schedule A, and an ultimately profitable investment.

Council tenants generally have lower incomes than owner-occupiers. Yet total subsidies to the council sector are much lower than the total of mortgage tax-relief; and the gap will continuously widen as a result of the Housing Finance Act. The private tenant, though he suffers by far the worst from insecurity, does now at least have the new rent allowance; for this much the Government deserves credit.

How can we make the system fairer? Firstly, for those on the lowest incomes, a national system of rebates and allowances is right. But it must be financed out of general taxation and not, as the Tories intend, largely from the rents of better-off council tenants.

Secondly, aid to the owner-occupier must be contained, for otherwise its inexorable growth (like food subsidies in the late 1940s) will bust the Exchequer: and it must be redistributed away from the rich towards those who cannot now afford a mortgage. People in my party often say that housing is a social service. It is not—it only has a social service *element;* and this does not embrace a home in Millionaires' Row or a weekend country house. Housing aid should not be indiscriminate. A limit should therefore be fixed on the amount of mortgage which attracts relief; no relief should be given on second homes; and the whole system should be assimilated to the option mortgage scheme to make it both less costly and less regressive.

Thirdly, we should aim at a broad equality of aid as between owner-occupier and tenant. The superficially logical ways of achieving this are unfortunately open to strong objection. It is sometimes suggested, for example, that rent should be offset against tax in the same way as mortgage interest. But this, like all tax allowances, would be highly regressive; and it would absorb in a most inefficient manner almost all the money available for council subsidies.

The idea of a universal housing allowance to replace all existing tax-relief and subsidies has been much canvassed recently. This would have the advantage of avoiding individual means-testing. But, on the evidence which I have so far seen, it would tend to help the better-off tenant more than the worse-off and the established owner-occupier more than the new or recent buyer.

Perhaps a refinement of the tax credit scheme may ultimately produce an answer. But for the moment we must rest on the crude but effective maxim that help to the rented sector should be broadly comparable in total to that available to the owner-occupier, and that it should be directed towards the people and the areas of greatest need. It would therefore not take the form of a universal indiscriminate subsidy; it would be embodied in four main subsidies—to rent rebates and allowances, high-cost high-rent areas, slum clearance and urban renewal, and municipalization.

Equality is not only a matter of finance; it is also a matter of social status. Nobody can pretend that the council tenant's standing in the community is as high as that of the owner-occupier; he still evokes a certain whiff of the welfare and second-class citizenship. This is partly due to the pervasive feeling, deplorably fostered by Conservatives, that renting is somehow morally inferior to buying. But it is also due to some strictly objective factors.

I have described these in previous *Guardian* articles, and proposed ways in which the council tenant can be given more choice, more variety, more community services, more security, and more democracy. Here I will only reiterate that tenants' rights and participation in management must form a central feature of our housing policy.

An Opposition is foolish to commit itself to excessively detailed policies; it lacks the knowledge and resources to test and check its suppositions and assumptions. But I believe that these articles provide the proper framework for an effective, credible and equitable Labour housing policy.

Part Three
The Environment

12 *Protecting the Environment*

Originally published in the Sunday Times *on June 25th 1972. It was written as an assessment of the results of the United Nations Conference on the Human Environment in Stockholm, which Anthony Crosland attended as a member of the British delegation.*

Cynics had long ago, and especially after the disaster of UNCTAD III at Santiago, written off the Stockholm Conference on the Human Environment as a futile exercise. They were wrong. It was a heartening success—and a liberating experience, since it freed us from the *either-or* syndrome so rampantly popular in the rich Western world.

The immediate results—the Action Plan, the new U.N. Environmental Agency and Fund, the final Declaration—have been sufficiently described. They are extremely important; and the impressive British delegation contributed substantially to them.

But, even more important in the long run, Stockholm finally brought the environmental debate down to reality. Until then it had been largely a dialogue of the deaf. The rich countries were talking about one problem, the poor about another. Both were talking to themselves.

In Britain, for example, as press and television pundits preached endlessly of ecological disaster and the need for zero-growth, the poor were scarcely permitted to eavesdrop, let alone participate. The debate in consequence had a trivial and even frivolous character; for the consequences of zero-growth to the less well-off were never seriously examined.

In Stockholm, however, the poor, in the shape of the developing countries, were present in force; and they put their contrary viewpoint with vociferous passion. 'Poverty', said Mrs Gandhi in the most eloquent speech of the conference, 'is the greatest polluter of all.' Speaker after speaker stressed that for two-thirds of the world's population the human environment was dominated by poverty, malnutrition and misery; and the most urgent task for mankind was to solve these immediate and formidable problems. In the words of the Jamaican rapporteur, 'the priority of the developing countries is development; a philosophy of "no growth" is absolutely unacceptable.'

Yet the education was a two-way process. Many developing countries came to Stockholm deeply suspicious, convinced that the environmental issue was a devious excuse for the rich countries to pull the ladder up behind them. They had not the slightest intention of remaining quaint Arcadian places, romanticized by tourists from the West.

They became increasingly aware, however, that the dangers of *uncontrolled* growth—to the countryside, to wildlife, to plant species, to the environment generally—were not figments of the imagination; they were real and serious. While it would always make sense for a poorer country to accept more pollution, whether from D.D.T. or smoking factories, than a richer one, there was no need to copy all the worst mistakes that the developed world had made in the course of its own ruthless industrial revolution.

Fortunately, there is no reason why they should; for there is no necessary conflict between growth and the environment. Contrary to what the doomwatch school assert, we are not in an *either-or* situation where we have to choose between the two. Growth does not inevitably mean a worse environment; more often it is a condition of a better one. I take the four critical problems discussed at Stockholm: poverty, population, pollution and resource depletion.

Firstly, the poverty, squalor and deprivation which are still the normal condition of much of mankind can only be banished by economic growth. Certainly we must redistribute wealth both between and within nations; but the world also needs a massive increase in total production. This was the bitter cry from every developing country at Stockholm; and only the callously selfish will resist it.

Secondly, population—an exponential increase in population would of course at some point calamitously exhaust some finite resource, food, water or ultimately space; and a few parts of the world already suffer from desperate over-population. We cannot share the complacency displayed at Stockholm by China and other countries with large virgin lands.

But an exponential increase is most unlikely. For it seems an invariable rule that as living-standards rise beyond a certain point, fertility rates decline. Most developed countries are now within sight of a stable population; and a few of the more prosperous developing countries have also experienced a dramatic fall in their birthrates in recent years. Far from being anti-growth, therefore, we should do all we can to help the poorer countries raise their living-standards. This is the most effective contribution (since it is not much good just instructing poor people to have fewer babies) which we can make to the world population problem.

Thirdly, pollution—uncontrolled growth means more pollution of every kind, more smoke, noise, effluent, garbage. But growth need not be uncontrolled—this is the heart of the whole matter—and the cost of pollution-control is smaller than is often imagined. Japan, for example, is now making prodigious efforts to repair the hideous ravages of past uncontrolled expansion; yet the rate of growth has scarcely been affected. In developing countries, with far less damage to undo, the problem is wholly manageable; Mr McNamara, head of the World Bank, estimates that pollution-control can be built into development projects at an additional cost of only 2 to 3 per cent.

And in some ways growth will ease the problem. It makes it simpler to find the money needed e.g. for sewage treatment or waste disposal; it hastens the substitution of modern pollution-free plant for old-fashioned polluting plant; and it facilitates the technological developments which will, though at a cost, eventually give us pollution-free cars and quiet aero-engines.

It is the fourth problem which excites the most violent controversy. The futurologists of the Club of Rome maintain that continued growth at the present rate will soon deplete irreplaceable natural resources of energy and minerals. Most economists are highly sceptical, believing that new discoveries, recycling and the use of substitutes will keep us supplied for the foreseeable future.

At the moment, we wholly lack the knowledge or techniques to say which school of thought is right. Certainly disaster is not round the corner, for most materials are now in excess supply, painfully so for the developing countries which produce them. We therefore should not be blackmailed, by apocalyptic visions of instant catastrophe, into accepting the first solution offered. We have time to find a reasoned answer; and it should be a priority for the new U.N. Agency to pursue this question in much more rigorous detail than has so far been attempted. Meanwhile, while we should not indulge in facile optimism, there is still less cause for premature defeatism.

I believe that these views represent the broad consensus of Stockholm. Growth remains vital to deal with both poverty and population. It may be inhibited at some future date; but so far there are neither clear facts nor rigorous analysis to support this fear. Meanwhile it can and must be strictly planned in the interests of the environment. Given such control, there need be no conflict between the two.

So we can move away from the recent sterile argument of growth versus anti-growth, and resume the real argument. How do we use and direct our growth? What should be its composition? How do we distribute it between different groups and different uses? This is the fundamental stuff of democratic political debate.

In Britain, there is already a profound disagreement between

Left and Right about the distribution of resources. Socialists believe that a greater share should go to the communal goods of health, education and the social services, and are willing to accept higher public expenditure and taxation for this purpose. (It is often forgotten by those who, like the Duke of Edinburgh, speak contemptuously of G.N.P. as the new 'graven image', that these expenditures count in G.N.P. just as fully as material consumer goods. So, if it comes to that, do paying visitors to Windsor Castle, the ticket money taken by Leeds United or Sadlers Wells, or a refit to the Royal Yacht *Britannia*.)

As to the environment, we have first a world responsibility — to allocate sufficient funds to foreign aid, to avoid using pollution fears as a protectionist device to limit trade, and to play a leading part in the post-Stockholm U.N. activities.

On the domestic front, a Labour policy for the environment will show a special concern for the goal of greater equality. Environmental benefits and detriments are most unevenly distributed. It is the less well-off who work and live in the worst environment; the rich can purchase a good environment for themselves.

Thus the less well-off work in a factory environment which is occasionally dreadful, often hideously noisy, usually dreary and unattractive. They live in crowded towns and cities, often in bad housing, usually with inadequate social facilities, always with too little space. They are almost invariably the sufferers from new urban motorways, inadequate public transport and the depredations of vainglorious developers. Their environment must have the first priority.

But naturally the problem goes far wider. It embraces pollution of all forms, control of the motor car, conservation of historic buildings, the design of housing estates, land-use planning to conserve the countryside, and so on.

Environmental goals should be particularly apt for the Labour movement, for they require policies and attitudes which come most easily to a left-wing Party—high public expenditure, social control, strict land-use planning, the elevation of community interests over developers' profits, a bias in favour of public transport, and a concern for industrial democracy (which should play a central role in improving the working environment). It was no accident that the Labour Government produced the first systematic survey of environmental pollution in its notable White Paper of May 1970.[1]

Labour's object is neither to limit growth (which would in any case be ludicrous in Britain, where we find it hard to grow at all) nor manically to pursue the private and material side of growth. It is to use growth to achieve the basic goals. So Labour must build the environmental factor into every economic decision. It must impregnate its thinking, especially its thinking about the less well-off.

13 *The Folly of Foulness*

Originally published in the Guardian, *on April 28th, 1971. The Government subsequently adopted the name of Maplin for the Foulness site.*

The Government have made a monumental blunder over the third London Airport. In choosing Foulness, they have committed hundreds of millions of pounds to building the wrong airport in the wrong place at the wrong time. They have made what is probably the most wasteful investment-decision of the century. Yet by ignoring economics, they have not protected the environment. Their claim to have taken the decision on environmental grounds is false.

For the first argument against Foulness is that it represents, as even Professor Buchanan[1] conceded, a 'severe loss' in environmental terms—of unspoiled coastline, sailing facilities and wildlife. If one includes noise as an environmental factor, as of course one should, Foulness will, for reasons I give later, cause a greater *total* noise nuisance than any other possible site.

Secondly, Foulness will involve the destruction of more homes than any other site. One has heard endlessly and rightly about the houses which would be destroyed by an airport at Cublington, but when one takes into account the need for new access motorways, Foulness will mean far more homes and families disrupted by bulldozers than would Cublington. But then of course they will be largely working-class homes, so they apparently count for less.

Thirdly, if, as the Government appear to envisage, an airport at Foulness is to be combined with a major seaport (for which, incidentally, no serious case has been made out) the resultant overcrowding and urbanization in South-East Essex would, as Professor Buchanan himself recognizes, be wholly unacceptable in regional planning terms. Fourthly, Foulness involves a serious safety-risk from birdstrike; and so great an authority as Lord Kings Norton regards this in itself as a sufficient argument against the site.

Fifthly, the additional costs of building at Foulness are enormous. I am not talking of subtle cost-benefit calculations of businessmen's time. I am talking of real economic resources required for building the airport and the road and rail links to it, resources that might otherwise be used in building schools or hospitals or houses.

Lastly, an airport at Foulness will prove, as I said in Parliament, 'the white elephant of the century'. No amount of differential pricing or restrictions on the use of other airports will persuade the airlines to use it; they will go to Continental airports instead. The result will be, not only a stupendous waste of money, it will also, in the end, mean a continuous build-up of traffic at Heathrow, Gatwick and Luton.

For the Government of the day, unable to force the airlines to use an airport they reject, yet alarmed by the loss of traffic and invisible earnings to the Continent, will gradually lift the restrictions at these airports; and the noise-nuisance will be even worse than it is today.

Why then did the Government choose Foulness in the face of these overwhelming objections? Negatively, of course, they were scared off the inland sites by the rich and powerfully organized pressure-groups, by the environmental lobby, which scandalously rushed into print before even reading the Roskill report, and generally by strong Tory feelings in both the Commons and the Lords.

In fact I think they were right on balance to reject the Roskill inland sites. The puzzle is why, having done so, they assumed there was no alternative to choosing Foulness. For there *is* an alternative. But it would involve a short period of further thought and study. This prospect no doubt excited the relentless opposition of civil servants who felt they had been round and round this course for ten years or more, and I well recall the strength of such feelings from the days when I determined to revoke the Stansted decision. If one adds to their opposition, Mr Heath's passion for superficially bold decisions, it is clear that Ministers lost their nerve and opted for the immediately popular choice.

But the alternative is greatly preferable in terms equally of the environment, of cost and of national aviation policy. It emerges as soon as one asks the basic question: what is the timing of the need for a four-runway third London Airport? This, after all, was the first question in the much-criticized Roskill terms of reference.

The answer is that there is no foreseeable need for such an airport at all. This was the critical conclusion to come out of the Roskill Commission (though they did not of course intend it as such). They showed that a third runway would not be completed at Foulness until 1998, and that a fourth runway would not, on their traffic forecast, be required even in the first decade of the next century.

But one is, by this time, in the realm of fantasy. It is meaningless to predict the need for conventional runways in the year 2000. One does not know what kinds of transport will be being used by then—STOL or VTOL[2] or new forms of surface transport. One can have no idea what the regional arguments will be—whether additional runways, if needed, would be better placed not in the South-East but in some other part of the country.

Certainly some additional conventional capacity will be needed in the South-East by the middle 1980s. It would be imprudent planning to assume that by then STOL will take up the whole increase in traffic. Moreover there must be extra capacity to relieve the pressure on Heathrow, Gatwick and Luton. Without it, there would be both an intolerable noise-burden at these airports and the risk of a total traffic snarl-up.

But no case has been made out for four additional runways

in the South-East. And even if it did turn out, which I believe most unlikely, that four more conventional runways would be needed by some time in the twenty-first century, the only price to be paid for not choosing a four-runway site now would be that two airports would have to be built with two runways each. This is no doubt less economical, but it would be far better than closing all the other options now.

If one rejects the case for choosing a potential four-runway site, an alternative policy unfolds. It has two aspects. Firstly, one should look for a site which would be suitable for an altogether more modest one- or two-runway airport. As it will cater mainly for charter and inclusive tour flights, it could be farther away from London than any of the Roskill inland sites.

It should ideally be a coastal site, but one without the appalling drawbacks of Foulness. Several possible sites have been suggested by the British Airports Authority; and there are many to be found among those rejected by Roskill because they were not suitable for four runways. Lydd, Hurn, Dengia Flats and sites in the so-called Essex gap would all be candidates.

Secondly, there is now a somewhat greater margin of time than was previously assumed. This is clear both from the revised traffic forecasts and the Government's decision not to plan for even the first additional runway until 1980. This margin should be used to intensify work on STOL and on noise generally, including retro-fits on existing jet engines. STOL in particular is currently being starved of Government funds. An investment here, at an infinitesimal fraction of the extra cost of Foulness, would bring dramatically better results both environmentally and economically.

The Government, alas, are ignoring this invaluable breathing space, and condemning the country instead to the horrors of a vast new international airport at Foulness. Their decision is not, as many commentators have glibly assumed, a triumph for the environment over economics. The alternative solution is much to be preferred on environmental as well as economic grounds.

But it would involve a short further delay, and the Government have preferred the immediately popular decision, which is also superficially firm and bold. Unfortunately quick and 'bold' solutions are so often a product of muddled thinking, surrender to pressure-groups and a palsied reluctance to sit down and think a problem through.

Such is the case with Foulness. For once, my hopes rest with the Treasury. They will surely become increasingly horrified by the hideous cost of the project, and bring the chopper down on it in some future bout of economy cuts. And for once I shall applaud them.

L

14 *The Future of Central London*

Speech delivered in the House of Commons on June 26th, 1972.

We have chosen this second half of a Supply Day to discuss Piccadilly, Covent Garden and all other schemes affecting the centre of London. We have chosen it extremely fortunately, because we read in today's evening papers of yet another scheme affecting the heart of central London, Piccadilly Mark II, a scheme which differs in certain respects from its immediate predecessor in that it has ten trees and a waterfall, but nevertheless one still based on the same unacceptable principles. What is more, like its predecessor, it has been cooked up behind locked doors, between Westminster City Council and private developers, it is wholly subservient to developers' profits, and it shows not the slightest interest in the wishes of the public. We believe that it is high time that Parliament, representing the public, debated what is happening to central London.

I shall not personally concentrate in detail on either Piccadilly or Covent Garden. Instead, I shall try to examine the total effect of all current plans, as far as they are known, on the character of the centre of London.

I intend to make my remarks under four heads. The first is that all the current schemes will generate additional employment in central London, especially office employment. The Covent Garden scheme will generate an extra 6,000 jobs. Piccadilly plus Artillery Mansions will generate an extra 3,000 to 4,000 office jobs. There is a proposed new development for an office block at Cambridge Circus, with one and a half times the capacity of Centre Point. Then there is Millbank, where the new proposals of the Crown Estates Commissioners will result in an extra 400,000 sq. ft. of offices. There is the Hatton Garden plan, again for more offices, and so on and so on.

Surely this goes wholly counter to the policy of successive Governments to disperse and decentralize office employment out of central London—ideally to the development and intermediate areas, which need jobs so badly, but to the extent that that is not possible, at least to chosen centres of expansion in outer London and the outer parts of the South-East region. This is precisely why the previous Conservative Administration set up the Location of Offices Bureau, though it is curious that its chairman at the moment should also be vice-chairman of Westminster City Council's planning committee. It was in order to achieve this that the Labour Government introduced the system of office development permits. This dispersal was the whole object of the strategic plan for the South-East, which has been rightly and strongly praised by the Secretary of State on many occasions. The absence of a proper dispersal policy has been the object of continuous criticism levelled at the Greater London Development Plan.

I admit freely that there are considerable practical difficulties in the way of this dispersal. I was not at all satisfied with the point that Government policy had reached when we left office in June 1970. But surely the objectives at any rate are clear. The policy of dispersing office employment out of central London is designed both to increase the volume and variety of employment in other parts of the country, with desperate unemployment problems, and also to reduce and relieve the congestion, the higher densities and the commuting, which a high level of office employment in central London inevitably produces.

If there has to be more office development in central London it seems extraordinary to put it in Piccadilly, Covent Garden and Pimlico and not at the main-line London termini, where British Rail would love to have it to help its ailing financial position. So my first objection to these new plans is that they drive a coach and horses through any sensible policy for the distribution of office employment.

My second objection to these plans is that Piccadilly and Covent Garden especially will both generate a significant increase in road traffic. Both positively provide for a 50 per cent increase in road traffic over 1960 levels. This, surely, is incredible planning.

The road proposals for Piccadilly and Covent Garden are based on a road strategy which is years old and now totally obsolete. They are based on a Ministry of Transport road strategy dating back to 1963 and, I regret to say, continued by the Labour Government. The strategy is not only ten years' old, it long pre-dates the Greater London Development Plan, which indeed makes no reference to it. Paragraph 7 of the Development Plan says,

> The task of planning central London's road system within the new conditions has yet to be more fully tackled and the developing structure of central London would largely depend on the secondary network throughout the area enclosed by Ringway One.[1]

In other words, no decision can conceivably be taken about either the Piccadilly or Covent Garden road proposals until the results of the G.L.D.P. inquiry are known.

There must be a traffic plan for the whole of central London which says which streets are to be mainly for road traffic and which are to be for the pedestrians. Until that plan has been formulated certainly no major increase in traffic densities should be allowed.

What is even more important than that is that since 1963, when the strategy was laid down, there has been a huge shift in public attitudes towards road traffic in city centres. We realize more clearly than we did a decade ago the appalling cost of a continuous increase in private road traffic in terms of noise, fumes, congestion, discomfort, the run-down of public transport and the need for more and more demolition of more and more homes to make way for the enlarged roads.

Even in terms of traffic management it is now seen more clearly that it does not work and that all that happens with traffic schemes is that the snarl-up is shifted a few miles ahead. The most dramatic recent example of that has been the effect of Westway in creating an almost continuous snarl-up in the busy rush hour period on the Edgware Road flyover. Time and time again this has been found to be a self-defeating process. That is why in every city in the western world the trend is in the opposite direction. Two of the working-parties set up by the Secretary of State to prepare for the Stockholm Conference on the Human Environment also showed a strong trend of opinion in the opposite direction. The whole emphasis now is on priority for buses and bus-only lanes, on flat-fare and other schemes for public transport, on restraint on the private motorist and his exclusion altogether from certain streets—as the Secretary of State and I saw in Stockholm recently, particularly the street containing all the pornshops: whether that was a coincidental decision I do not know—and generally a greater emphasis on public transport.

I am glad that even the Conservative-controlled Greater London Council has now seen the light with its proposals for Oxford Street. I am particularly delighted that the Labour opposition group, likely to take power in May, has produced a radical plan for improving public transport and restraining private transport in the London area.

But the Piccadilly and Covent Garden schemes have been produced as though none of this change of opinion had occurred. It is not surprising that Sir Richard Way, Chairman of London Transport, said of the Piccadilly scheme in a letter to my Hon. Friend the Member for Walthamstow, West (Mr Deakins), 'The present proposals appear to reflect outdated planning concepts.' It might be worth pulling Piccadilly down, though I doubt it, to make way for an up-to-date traffic plan, but it is certainly not acceptable to pull it down to make way for an outdated traffic plan.

My third objection is that many of the schemes under discussion are destroying the character and sense of community of important parts of traditional central London. Of course these are subjective matters. One either likes Piccadilly Circus as it now stands, as I happen to do, except for the traffic, or one agrees with Mr Cubitt who said that Piccadilly Circus is 'little more than a down-at-heel, neon-lit slum'. But it is not in dispute that there are strong communities which are threatened by some of these development plans, most obviously that of Covent Garden. And as to the character of central London, the majority of Londoners, if one were to ask their opinion, which one does not, would say that they do not like the change of character which these grandiose, gigantic, comprehensive development plans produce.

I can list what there will be more of, after one of these schemes, and what there will be less of, after one of these schemes. After one of these schemes there is, invariably, less working-class housing, fewer small shops, clubs and restaurants, less variety of architectural scale, less mixture of income and occupation, fewer traditional landmarks and generally less community, character and humanity. Those are the things that traditionally go. What there is more of, is traffic, concrete, tower-blocks, upper-deck pedestrian ways and, in the process, invariably much higher rents and much higher house prices.

This is not what Londoners want—except the property developers. There is now beginning to be a violent reaction against this type of comprehensive redevelopment. The irony is that both the Conservative and the Labour Governments have been extremely sensitive to this reaction in another sector, namely housing. In the 1969 Housing Act, the Labour Government, and now supported by the present Government—I pay tribute to the Secretary of State for this—and by the great majority of local authorities, put a much greater emphasis in housing on improvement, conservation and rehabilitation as against massive demolition, clearance and redevelopment. Similarly, there is much more emphasis, today, on low-rise building and a variety of scales and much less emphasis on enormous tower blocks. I believe that the same shift of emphasis is needed when we are talking about whole areas. I do not mean that there should be no change of any kind. There must be some piecemeal improvement to stop blight and general rundown. But the improvement should be a piecemeal, gradual and sensitive one and not these vast schemes for comprehensive redevelopment.

But the trouble is, and here I make a point which obviously must divide the two sides of the House, that piecemeal improvement is infinitely less attractive to the private developers because it brings them much less profit and site-return than total demolition and rebuilding. There is an absolutely direct conflict between private profit and the public interest. There is a situation in which the objective will not be achieved without the public ownership of development land.

My fourth objection is that what is going on in central London is the antithesis of any proper planning. There is a muddle of piecemeal proposals. This is all very well and often positively desirable if we are discussing a single site, but it is disastrous if applied to central London as a whole. The present position is almost incredible. There are wholly separate plans at present for Covent Garden. There is Piccadilly Mark I. There is now Piccadilly Mark II, just produced out of a hat. There is a plan for a Trafalgar Square pedestrian precinct. There is still, I assume, I do not know what has happened to it, a Whitehall redevelopment plan which was prepared years ago by Sir Leslie Martin and Professor Sir Colin Buchanan. For my part, though, if that plan were sunk without trace I should not be sorry.

There is the Grosvenor Estate plan for Mayfair and Belgravia. A few days ago a new plan was announced by the Crown Estates Commissioners, a £20 millions plan, for the twenty-three acres of the Millbank Estate. All these plans involve the inevitable increase in office space, the inevitable conference centre, the inevitable increase in road traffic and the inevitable increases in rents and house prices. None of these separate plans is related to any other. They are not drawn together. They are not presented as part of a coherent view of what sort of central London we want. They are not even produced by a single planning authority.

In passing, I must say that the way in which the G.L.C. has abdicated responsibility for Piccadilly is a disgrace. It was simply part of a horse-dealing agreement with Westminster City Council, that if the G.L.C. kept out of Piccadilly, Westminster would keep out of Covent Garden. That is not the way in which the affairs of a great capital city should be managed.

Not only are these plans not related to each other, but they are not related in any way to what may come out of Mr Frank Layfield's G.L.D.P. inquiry[2] and the Minister's decision on it. After all, the Minister will have to take decisions in the light of the panel's report on office employment policy, on densities for central London, on road traffic schemes in central London and on the whole character of central London. The decisions which the Minister, rightly, will have to take on these matters, could easily totally destroy all the assumptions on which the Piccadilly, Covent Garden and other schemes are based. That is a farcical position.

Even more serious, without waiting for the results of the various inquiries, now in process, developments are going ahead or are announced, which will pre-empt the Minister's decision, and in the process will determine the character of central London as a whole, while we can do virtually nothing about it.

I take the Covent Garden area as an example. There is the Hazlemere development at the back of Drury Lane, the demolition of the Odhams Press building, and the proposal to which I briefly referred, Cambridge Circus, with Trentishoe Mansions, which I am told if improved could house a hundred people, now having their tenants cleared out. The last one has now been cleared out, and the site is to be used for a development by Town and City Properties, a nineteen-storey office block with an office employment capacity one and a half times that of the long-empty Centre Point. This is a development which would surely totally destroy the character of Charing Cross Road, with all its bookshops, which I should have thought would be a great loss to central London. I am happy to say that the Camden Council is fighting this development. I wish them every success.

But similar developments are going on in the rest of central London. For instance, in Hatton Garden there is a new plan for the Gamages site by Town and City Properties, again more offices, higher rents, and demolition of existing small traders' premises. At this moment, at the corner of Piccadilly and Hamilton Place, at Hyde Park Corner, a group of nineteenth-century houses is being demolished to make way for an hotel tower block for Pan-Am and B.O.A.C. I was all for encouraging luxury hotels in London four or five years ago. Indeed, it was one of my schemes that gave such an incentive. But is it still necessary to have a large number of additional luxury as opposed to second-class hotels in central London? I doubt it.

Then there is Petty France and Queen Anne's Mansions practically across the way. Most of us discovered, almost by accident, a proposal for a huge tower block on that site to be designed by Sir Basil Spence. Whether we want any more contributions by Sir Basil Spence to London's skyline is, I should have thought, a matter for considerable doubt.

What is particularly objectionable is that much of this is going on in a secret, wheeler-dealer, hole-in-the-corner kind of way. Piccadilly Mark I was produced without its ever going to the Westminster Planning Committee. Piccadilly Mark II appeared in the evening newspapers tonight for the first time without anyone ever having seriously discussed it. There was the vulgar horse-trading between Westminster Council and the Land Securities Investment Trust over Artillery Mansions. I should like to hear the comments of Lady Dartmouth and her

Stockholm working-party on how these matters are being conducted, in view of all that she and her party said about public participation and the need for public choice in these matters.

I believe with passion that it is now time to call a halt. It is time to stop this piecemeal hacking away at our city. It is time to say to the G.L.C., to Westminster City Council, to Land Securities Investment Trust, to Town and City Properties, to the lot of them, 'Gentlemen, we've had enough. We, the people of London, now propose to decide for ourselves what sort of city we want to live in.'

Only the Minister can make this wish effective. What should he do? I believe that as a minimum he should call for a stop to all major developments in central London at least till Mr Layfield and his panel have reported on the G.L.D.P. I do not mean that everything should be totally stopped. Of course, there must be a continuing process of renovation, restoration and the occasional replacement of existing buildings. I am speaking about major schemes of the Piccadilly or Covent Garden variety.

It must be clear that sensible decisions cannot be taken on any of these individual schemes until Mr Layfield's views on the road network, office employment and all those matters concerning London as a whole have been heard. But I do not think that will be enough because the Layfield inquiry goes very wide and covers the greater London area, which has a population as great as some of the regions. It may not, therefore, go into detail on the historic centre of London which we are discussing tonight. A view of central London must be taken in the light of the strategy for greater London which emerges from the G.L.D.P. inquiry.

How do we get a total view of the kind of central London that we want? One alternative, I suppose, would be to use the Central London Planning Conference. I do not know how many Hon. Members until recently, or perhaps even now, have been familiar with this body. I am ashamed to say that I have not been very familiar with it. It is a conference which has as its constituents a number of the central London boroughs. I see that it has recently approved a proposal for the preparation of a co-ordinated plan for the central area, to be called 'The Advisory Plan for Central London'.

I welcome its awareness that there must be a plan for central London as a whole, and I am, as the Secretary of State knows, a consistent defender of local democracy. But we are not tonight discussing simply a local Government problem. We are not discussing the centre of Grimsby, but the centre of our capital city. I discussed the centre of Grimsby on Sunday, when I had to excoriate Labour, as well as Conservative councillors, for pulling down every building which was worth preserving in Grimsby. But I doubt whether the Central London Planning Conference is the right way to treat the matter now before us. We must treat it as a national problem.

I propose to the Secretary of State, therefore, that once he has the report of the G.L.D.P. inquiry, he should set up a planning inquiry commission under Section 62 of the 1968 Town and Country Planning Act, to examine in the light of the G.L.D.P. strategy all major schemes affecting the historic centre of London, the Commission to sit in public and to include lay members of the public. It should be deliberately designed to stimulate the most intense public discussion and debate. It is obvious that this would mean, let us say, a two-year delay or moratorium on all these plans. I would regard that as an admirable result. The Secretary of State quite rightly was willing to accept a two-year moratorium in the case of London's dockland, so if it was right to freeze development effectively for two years, in order at the end to get a better plan as a result of a better survey for dockland, it surely must be right also for the historic centre of the country's capital.

If the Secretary of State rejects that, I do not mind what method he uses provided he achieves the objective, which is to prohibit further destruction until the public have taken a view about what sort of place they want Central London to be, and until the public have told us whether they share the vision of central London, which I certainly do not, that is presented by Mr Cubitt, Mr Prendergast, Sir Charles Forte and Sir Harold Samuel.

If the Minister takes the opposite view and allows these plans to go ahead, a very dangerous mood will develop amongst Londoners. There already is a mood of helpless resentment at the inability to stop these damned developments, and this may turn into a mood of active resentment. People will not have London continuously mutilated in this way for the sake of property development and the private motorist. They will not have an endless number of Centre Points and an endless number of uniform, monolithic, comprehensive redevelopments which break up communities and destroy the historic character of the city.

In conclusion, I will take a liberty, which I do not often take, of reading something I wrote in a book which I called aptly *The Conservative Enemy* and which I wrote ten years ago.

> Excited by speculative gain, the property developers furiously rebuild the urban centres with unplanned and aesthetically tawdry office blocks; so our cities become the just objects of world-wide pity and ridicule for their architectural mediocrity, commercial vulgarity and lack of civic or historic pride.

I believe that is even more true today. The Secretary of State, like myself, has returned from the United Nations Conference on the Human Environment at Stockholm. Let him take the opportunity we have provided tonight, to say loud and clear, and once and for all, that both Parties place the human environment above the profits of the Land Securities Investment Trust.

15 *Reform of Local Government*

Speech delivered in the House of Commons on February 18th, 1970, introducing the Labour Government's White Paper on Reform of Local Government in England (Cmnd, 4276). For Mr Crosland's criticisms of the alternative proposals of the Conservative Government see Hansard for May 19th, 1971, cols. 1292–1309.

The present system of local government dates in its essentials from the nineteenth century. We can all agree at least on two propositions: firstly, that tribute is due to those thousands of councillors and officers who have done so much to make the present system work; secondly, however, that this system has now become anachronistic.

There are today no fewer than 1,210 authorities administering local government services in England outside London; these 1,210 are split between 5 different types of authority, each with a different set of powers—79 county boroughs, 45 county councils, 227 non-county boroughs, 449 urban district councils, and 410 rural district councils.

County boroughs are of course all-purpose authorities, but all the others are only some-purpose authorities. The division of functions between them is not the result of any coherent plan, but has emerged over the years from a variety of separate decisions about individual services.

This patchwork effect is heightened by the great variety and illogicality in the size of authorities. There are 98 county districts, with populations ranging from 50,000 to 123,000; but as many as 42 out of the 79 county boroughs are also in this population range. This overlap is, to say the least, hard to defend when one remembers the big difference between the functions of county boroughs and county districts.

If one looks at the size of authorities responsible for particular services, one finds that the City of Birmingham, with a population of 1,100,000, and the smallest rural district, with a population of 1,500, are both housing authorities, with exactly the same responsibility for dealing with the housing problems of their areas.

Bootle, jammed tight up against Liverpool, has the full powers of a planning authority for an area of 5 square miles. Devon County Council has exactly the same planning powers, but for an area of more than 2,500 square miles.

This mosaic pattern produces fundamental weaknesses. The first stems from the division between town and country in the organization of services. This no longer bears any relation to reality. It is not that town and country have become identical, or that their interests have become identical. But they have become socially and economically interdependent, and their interests are intermeshed.

The towns need, and increasingly need, the countryside— for housing space, for leisure and for recreation. Indeed, they cannot breathe properly within their present borders. Those who live in the country increasingly work, shop and find their entertainment in the towns. And as the number of cars doubles in the next fifteen years, these links will grow still closer.

So to try to administer town and country separately for planning, transport and development, as happens today, becomes more and more impossible. There is not a county borough in England which can solve its housing and planning problems within its present boundaries. Nor can most rural districts claim to be self-contained when, as the last census showed, nearly half of those who live in rural districts work outside the district boundaries.

To have one planning authority for a county borough and another for the county around it means that each can deal with only part of a problem which ought to be seen as a single whole. Any new system must bring town and country together for planning purposes. I do not think that anyone who has thought about the matter seriously holds a contrary view.

The second weakness of the present system is that it separates services that should be administered together. County councils, although planning authorities, have no responsibility for housing: so although they can make plans they lack one of the most important means of carrying them out. The personal social services come under the county councils, but housing under the county districts—a division which the Seebohm Committee strongly criticized.

The third weakness is that many of the present authorities are too small. The Redcliffe-Maud Commission was very candid about the relationship between size and efficiency. It said quite plainly that no statistical relationship could be proved to exist. This was an important negative conclusion; it showed that there is not one single, optimum size for particular services. But that does not mean that we can wash our hands of the problem, and leave things as they are; not even the urban district councils and the rural district councils suggested that we could.

The weight of advice received by the Commission was that a population of about 250,000 is necessary for the effective provision of the main services. This is also the view of the Government. One can, of course, find authorities with smaller populations than this, which provide individual services at a high standard. But when one takes an overall view of the right size for authorities administering a wide range of services, we believe, and I shall return to this question later, that a minimum population in the region of 250,000 is required. This in itself involves a reshaping of the whole structure.

Lastly, the present system greatly confuses the public. When a person can walk along a city street and pass from one local authority area to another without knowing it; when he can find the offices of three distinct authorities—county council, borough or urban district council, and rural district council—

each with its separate jurisdiction, in the same country town; when he cannot understand why different authorities exercise different functions, it is hardly surprising if people do not know who is responsible for what service in which area. This confusion leads only too easily to apathy and indifference.

All this means that local government as a whole is too weak. Because there are so many different types of authority, each with its own national association, local government cannot speak to the central Government with a united voice. Because there are so many small authorities with limited resources, the central Government are forced to maintain checks on their performance that would be unnecessary if every authority commanded adequate resources. Because of the division between county councils and county boroughs, there is hardly an authority in the country which is responsible for an area that ought to be planned as a whole. Therefore, the central Government, under either party, are constantly having to intervene in planning decisions which local authorities should take for themselves.

When people complain about Government interference in local affairs, the fault is by no means wholly that of the Government. It is often that only the central Government can take the necessary action, because local authority resources and areas do not correspond with the scale of the job to be done. The trend towards centralization has occurred partly because our local government structure has remained fixed in an out-of-date mould.

It was a recognition of these weaknesses which led to the appointment of the Royal Commission. One should not forget now that the decision to set it up was generally—indeed, almost universally—applauded.

The evidence to the Commission reflected the feeling that radical change was essential. Virtually no one recommended that the status quo should be retained. Obviously, witnesses varied in the proposals they made, but the main bodies of opinion all suggested the union of town and country and a drastic reduction in the number of authorities. The Redcliffe-Maud Report[1] has been criticized as revolutionary. In fact, it did not go so far as some authoritative witnesses would have liked.

When we held our consultations on the Commission's report, there was, again, no serious argument in favour of keeping things as they are. The need for change is accepted. The debate is about what form it should take.

There cannot be a single right answer to the problem of how to organize local government. Reasonable men are bound to hold different views, the more so since we are not creating a new system from scratch but are reorganizing a system which has deep roots in history.

To begin with, there cannot be the same structure for the entire country. To impose a uniform system everywhere would do great violence to basic social and economic facts. What matters, in our increasingly mobile society, is the distribution of population, the pattern of employment, the system of communications, the journeys people make from home to work, the business and industrial links in an area, the pull of shopping centres and the way that people spend their leisure.

The more one looks at the map of England, the more one sees, as the Commission did, that these 'social and economic facts' point to different structures for different parts of the country. Many commentators have said the same. The Association of Municipal Corporations, which strongly favours the unitary principle, accepted the case for a two-tier authority in the areas round Birmingham, Liverpool and Manchester.

Mr Senior, who wrote the Memorandum of Dissent and who is generally an enthusiast for a two-tier system, accepted some unitary authorities. Again and again, people stressed that there must be flexibility—that to have the same system everywhere would be over-rigid and unrealistic. So like the Commission, we propose a structure which is part unitary and part two-tier.

Just as there are different views about structure, so there are

M

about the right size of authority. The fact is, again, that there is no one size which is uniquely right, while all others are wrong. People's views about size are often coloured by the particular services in which they are most interested. Planners go for the wide expanses, the city region or even the province.

Educationists also like large areas, in which every demand can be catered for, and every subject have its quota of specialist staff. In the personal social services, people used to prefer the small authority, whose members could be in intimate touch with those in need. This is much less so today. There has been a growing realization—strongly reinforced by the Seebohm Report[2]— of just how much expertise modern social services require, an expertise that must be organized in teams, to operate over sizeable areas if full use is to be made of their skills.

Though there is no uniquely right size or right structure, there must be certain basic principles. In the Government's view, they are as follows. Firstly, the areas of the new authorities must be large enough for planning. Secondly, to be able to afford the skilled manpower and other resources, needed to provide services of the highest standard, an authority should have a population, in our view, of no fewer than about 250,000. Thirdly, wherever possible, each authority should be responsible for all the services in its area.

'Unitary' may be an ugly word, but it conceals an important truth. Local government services interact on each other, and the links between them grow closer every year. An authority responsible for the full range of services can look at them all, in relation to each other, and to the needs of its area as a whole. It can work out a general policy for its area, and give each service the right role and the right priority. It can plan capital expenditure more sensibly, and co-ordinate investment in the different services to get the greatest benefit. There is also a great gain for the public understanding of local government, without which there can be no effective democracy.

Fourthly, however, an authority responsible for all services clearly should not be so large as to be unmanageable or un-responsive to the wishes of the electors. In our view, this means that it should not normally have a population of much over a million. There is no magic about this figure; perhaps there are areas where we might have gone rather more above it than we have. But it does mean that we are not creating the 'monster authorities' that some critics have talked about. Most of the unitary authorities would have populations of under half a million; Birmingham today has over 1 million. Only one, Sheffield and South Yorkshire, would have a bigger population than Birmingham—and it would be bigger by only 6,000.

In certain parts of the country, the size of the area to be planned as a whole produces a population well above this limit of 1 million, and so a unit that is too large for single-tier administration. The Commission found that this was the case round Liverpool, Manchester and Birmingham; and we concluded, for reasons given in the White Paper, that it was also the case in West Yorkshire and South Hampshire. In these areas, services must be divided between two tiers.

These, then, are the principles on which the White Paper structure is based—wherever practicable, unitary authorities with populations in the range from 250,000 to 1,000,000, but a two-tier metropolitan pattern around certain actual or potential conurbations.

I turn to functions. I do not need to spend time on the functions of the unitary authorities, since they will have statutory responsibility for the entire range of local government services in their areas.

We cannot achieve such simplicity in the metropolitan areas. But we can get away from the present situation in the counties, where services that ought to be administered together are administered separately; where responsibility for a parti-cular service, such as roads, is divided between different authorities; and where statutory schemes of 'delegation' mean that education, the social services and planning can be adminis-tered in different ways in different parts of a county.

Generally, we have accepted the Commission's views on the division of functions in metropolitan areas. Planning, transport, major development, general housing policy and the power to build houses in the interests of the whole area, are at the upper tier. The districts will be responsible for the other housing functions, all the local authority social services, and a large number of other services that are best administered at district level. This means that districts must be of a substantial size.

We have disagreed with the Commission on one major function. The Commission followed the Seebohm Committee in thinking that education and the personal social services should always be with the same authority: so it allotted them both to the metropolitan districts. We take a different view and have allotted education to the upper tier. This is not because we believe in size for its own sake in education. But there is a minimum size below which an education authority cannot provide, for example, specialist further education courses or teacher training, an adequate range of special schools, physical education facilities, computers or closed circuit television, and a full range of advisory and inspection staff.

The argument is especially strong in the field of further and higher education. It would really not make sense to divide responsibility for this between nine metropolitan districts in Selnec—I use the Commission's term—and seven in the West Midlands. In putting education at the upper tier we have, I think, the support of the great majority of educationists.

The main anxiety which has been expressed about the new structure, it is perhaps rather a group of anxieties, relates to the alleged size and remoteness of the new authorities, the reduction in the number of councillors, and the supposed weakening of truly local democracy. I sympathize greatly with these anxieties, but believe them to be unfounded.

First, remoteness—this might refer to a number of things. It might refer to accessibility of the town or county hall. The headquarter centres of the new areas will be for local decision, but there are obvious candidates, and a study of these shows

that out of a population of 38 million in England, outside
Greater London 35 million, over 90 per cent, will live within
20 miles of a likely centre.

It might refer to size. The largest proposed unitary area,
Exeter and Devon, covers 2,227 square miles. But this is less
than the existing administrative counties of Devon and the
West Riding, each responsible for major services and each
covering over 2,500 square miles.

It might refer to population. The largest proposed unitary
authority, Sheffield and South Yorkshire, will have a population
of 1,081,000. But this is less than the present populations of the
counties of Lancashire, West Riding, Kent and Essex. It is
only fractionally larger than that of the county borough of
Birmingham.

It might refer to representation—that is, the number of
electors whom each councillor represents. Even with a maximum of seventy-five members, and we do not accept this
maximum, the largest unitary authority, Sheffield and South
Yorkshire, would have, on average, one councillor for every
14,000 inhabitants.

But the present Kent and Lancashire County Councils have,
on average, one councillor for 19,000 inhabitants, the West
Riding one for 18,000, and individual constituencies go up to
30,000 or 40,000. And in none of the proposed metropolitan
areas would we approach the present ratio in the Greater
London Council of one elected member to 78,000 inhabitants.

I do not argue from all this that no problem of remoteness
exists; indeed, our proposals for district committees and local
councils, to which I come in a moment, are intended to meet
it. But I do argue that, contrary to much public comment, we
are not creating a new type of giant authority which has no
equivalent today. On the contrary, there are equivalents, and
interestingly they are to be found amongst the most highly
regarded of our present authorities.

Secondly, the number of elected members—it is not
in dispute that there will be a drastic fall in the number of

councillors exercising statutory responsibility for services. There are now about 32,000 councillors of county boroughs, county councils, non-county boroughs and urban and rural districts. There would be between 6,000 and 7,000 councillors on the new main authorities.

But there would be a drastic fall under any proposed scheme for reorganization. Take, for example, the proposals of the Urban and Rural District Councils Associations, supported perhaps by some Hon. Members and generally thought to be much less radical than our own. The U.D.C.A., which wanted a two-tier system throughout England, thought that the second-tier authorities should normally have a population of 60,000. But only 55 of the present 1,086 county districts have a population of over 60,000. The R.D.C.A. was even more draconian. It suggested that a second-tier authority should have a population of over 100,000. On this basis, only four existing second-tier authorities out of 1,086 would be big enough.

I do not quote these figures to disparage in any way the arguments put forward by these associations. I quote them only to show what a drastic reduction in the number of councils and councillors is involved even in proposals which may seem conservative when compared with our own White Paper. It is part of the price we must pay for any serious reform.

But whatever its precise extent, the fall in the number of councillors is a serious matter. We have tried to mitigate it by suggesting that members of local councils should belong to district committees and take part there in the running of main services. Our proposal to create two more two-tier areas will also slightly increase the number of councillors with operational responsibility. Moreover, as I have already said, we do not accept the Commission's recommendation that no authority should have more than seventy-five members. In our view this is a matter which needs further study.

Thirdly, the question of local democracy—this is a term to which different people attach different meanings. In the *Daily Mail* recently, Mr Longland, one of the members of the

Commission, said that when people spoke about local democracy what they were really talking about was holding on to power. Now I think that this was unfair. But it is perhaps true, that in local government, as elsewhere, people tend, sincerely and naturally, to equate institutions that they know and love with genuine democracy and to regard all other institutions as its enemy. I do not think that in representative local government there is something which makes a small unit inherently more democratic than a big one.

Mr Longland made what is surely a valid point in his note of reservation when he said that it would be meaningless 'to claim that the Isle of Wight has been governed more democratically than Hertfordshire, or Rochdale than Birmingham'.

Nor must one idealize the extent of public interest or democratic participation in the present system. Only about 40 per cent of the electorate vote in local government elections. A study done by the Commission showed that only 13 per cent of people have ever contacted their local councillor; many, as we all know, contact their Member of Parliament instead. Nearly half the county councillors, and two thirds of rural district councillors, are returned unopposed. I say this, not to condemn the present state of affairs, but to show that we are not comparing some horrific future with a perfect and ideal present.

Nevertheless, the problem of local participation, even though this has not been solved under the present system, remains one of profound importance. For reasons I have given, I do not believe that the answer lies in having small, weak second-tier authorities exercising statutory functions. The statutory functions are best kept separate from the function of representing the local community and caring for the local environment.

This brings me to our proposals for local councils. I am not sure, incidentally, whether these proposals differ from those of the party opposite. I note that the Hon. Member for Worcester (Mr Peter Walker) has supported 'the principle of the existence of a bottom tier to look after genuinely local amenities'. I shall be glad to hear how he thinks this differs from our own proposals.

The Commission's proposals on the subject were widely misunderstood. But I have noticed, since the Commission's report was published, a growing awareness that unitary authorities must have local councils as their counterpart. I personally cannot conceive of a system in which there was no elected body at a more local level than that of the main authority. We cannot forbid Dover and Deal, Woodstock and Chipping Norton, King's Lynn and Cirencester, Clacton and Skegness, Warwick and Bury St. Edmunds to have a council of any kind. People in these places will want to make their voice heard on a proposal for a gasworks or a motorway; they will want to spend money on local amenities, a car park, a playing field, a local museum, a 'Come to Skegness' campaign; and they will want to make appointments to school governing bodies and other local bodies.

All these things we propose, as did the Commission, that local councils should be able to do. But I think that we have also improved on the Commission's proposals. True, we have rejected the suggestion that the larger councils should be able to play a part in some of the main statutory services. This would have brought back fragmentation of responsibility, confusion of the public, and all the unsatisfactory features of the two-tier system in an even worse form than now. Almost all informed commentators have agreed that on this point we are right.

But local councils must be involved in the work of the main authorities. We propose to achieve this through membership of district committees. In the new system, the main authorities would have to decentralize their administration, even if there were no local councils. But district committees will provide a method of decentralization that allows members of local councils to take a direct part in the operation of services.

But whereas the Commission thought that the areas of local councils should not be changed for a further five years, while the new system settled down, we think that changes should be made as soon as practicable after reorganization.

The problem of areas will not be acute for the smaller local councils. The village and the small or medium-sized town are usually communities in the sense that matters here. The problem arises in Sheffield and Bristol, Coventry and Hull.

When a town gets above, say, the 100,000 mark, it should be a matter for local decision whether it is represented by a single local council, or whether the different communities which compose it should each have their own local council. I personally hope that many of them will choose to have neighbourhood or community councils. Such councils might bring new people and fresh strength into local democracy.

There has been a massive growth recently of what I might call 'one-purpose' interest groups in local affairs. This is partly due to a vague but real discontent with the channels open to people to influence events, and perhaps an inchoate but often real demand for 'participation', if that word has not been over-used. I believe that neighbourhood councils could focus this in a constructive way.

I turn to the relationship between central and local government. The White Paper states that 'the Government believe unequivocally in greater freedom for local authorities within the framework of national policies laid down by Parliament.' I stress that last clause in view of certain comments on the alleged inconsistency between the declaration in the White Paper and the recent Education Bill. This is a matter which had better be cleared up.

No one has ever suggested that local government should be free to depart from major national objectives. The Redcliffe-Maud Commission was by no means tender towards central government. When it discussed the relationship between central and local government it always favoured the greatest possible freedom for local authorities. But it recognized, as everyone must, that national policies must have priority. It recognized 'the responsibility of central government to settle the policies

to be followed in the provision of services of national importance'. It said that local authorities 'must conform to current
national policies'.

No one seriously disputes this. In education, for example,
there are many matters which must be the concern of central
government. It is not suggested that local authorities should be
allowed to set the school-leaving age in their areas. We on this
side of the House believe that the abolition of the 11-plus
comes into the same category. It is an objective of national
policy, and should be declared as such by Parliament. There is
no inconsistency here.

Within the framework of national policies, the White
Paper makes positive proposals for giving local authorities
greater freedom from central control. With reorganization we
can get rid of detailed controls that have to be kept in force
when there are over 1,200 separate authorities. We propose,
and this will be much welcomed in the world of local government, to end the control of capital expenditure through the
tiresome medium of the individual loan sanction. And for
something like a quarter of local authority capital expenditures
we shall give authorities complete freedom to decide, within a
total figure, their own projects and their own priorities.

We also want authorities to have the greatest possible freedom to manage their own affairs, in the way they think best,
without being confined in a straitjacket of obsolete statutory
provisions, which require them to set up separate committees
for this purpose or that. For obvious reasons, this cannot apply
to the police, and the Seebohm Committee's recommendations
will call for special treatment. But we aim, to quote the words
of the White Paper, for 'a minimum of general rules and plenty
of experiment'.

We intend, moreover, to go beyond a mere relaxation of
controls, and to give local authorities a general power to
spend money for the benefit of their areas and inhabitants.
This is something they do not have at the moment—except in
the form of a power to spend the product of all of a penny rate.

These are serious and positive proposals; and if anyone doubts our intentions let me quote two specific decisions which have already been taken. Firstly, when we set up the four passenger transport authorities, we placed them in effect under the joint control of the local authorities, in the areas concerned, because we think and thought that decisions on public transport in the large conurbations are essentially a matter for local government. After reorganization, the P.T.A.s will be handed over entirely to a single local authority in each area; and, of course in London we have already handed over London Transport to the G.L.C.

Secondly, we took powers in the 1968 Planning Act for devolution to local authorities; and we have already used these powers in some places. After reorganization there will be automatic devolution to all the new planning authorities. These examples are both an earnest of our intentions and an illustration of how, if we can enlarge the size of authorities, we can also increase their powers.

I want, finally, to say a word about finance. It has been argued that reform of finance should logically precede decisions on structure. I do not agree. The logical course, and the right one, is to settle the structure, to decide on the size of areas and the allocation of resources, and then make the financial arrangements that are appropriate to the new structure. We cannot take sensible decisions on finance until we know, and unless we know, how many authorities there will be, of what size, with what functions, and what resources. The structure must determine the financial arrangements and not the other way round.

In any case, even the present financial arrangements, less than perfect though they are, would be adequate to sustain the new structure proposed in the White Paper. And, indeed, I doubt whether, in practice, any new study, and we have had plenty of studies both inside and outside Government in recent years, will lead to a wholly revolutionary new method of financing local government.

Following the decisions now taken on structure, the Government will publish a Green Paper setting out our detailed proposals for local government finance and taxation. There will have to be central grants under any system of local government, but no one likes the present situation, in which authorities depend on such grants for so much of their revenue. The Green Paper will, therefore, discuss possible supplementary sources of revenue for local authorities. But I must say now that the Government agree with the Commission that rates must remain the chief local tax.

Rates are certainly unpopular and in many ways unsatisfactory. But the present Government have taken a number of important steps to make them fairer and more palatable— payment by instalments, special relief for domestic ratepayers through the rate support grant, and rate rebates, for which the income limits will be raised on 1st October. I am sure, that with hard work and ingenuity, we can do still more to make them less regressive. But I am equally sure, as was the Commission, that they must remain the principal local tax.

To conclude, we are all agreed that a major reform of local government is needed. We are probably all agreed that there is no uniquely right solution which will satisfy everybody. Any solution will cause upheaval and disturbance. Any solution will be unpopular with some critics and in some parts of the country. Any solution will cause a large reduction in the number of councillors. So none of us who believes in reform can be, or should try to be, competitors for popularity; and those who differ from our proposals must spell out frankly the implications of their own.

I claim for our proposals that in their variety they fit the different needs of different parts of the country; that they create a pattern of main authorities better able to meet the public demand for efficient local services; that they create the possibility, in the local councils, of a virile and genuinely local democracy; and that they provide the necessary condition for greater freedom from central government control.

In the debate on the last major proposals for reform in 1888, the Prime Minister, Lord Salisbury, commending those proposals in the House of Lords, said that 'the evil of leaving things as they are seems to me much greater than any evil that could possibly come from the Bill.' I would put it today more positively. People want two things from local government: firstly, they want housing, education, the social services, transport and amenities to be provided at the highest possible standard; secondly, they want to make their voices heard loud and clear when those in authority propose things which offend their local feelings.

I claim that our proposals will, more effectively than either the present system or any proposed alternative, satisfy these two objectives.

Part Four
Education

16 Comprehensive Education

Speech delivered at the North of England Education Conference on January 7th, 1966.

I want to talk about comprehensive reorganization—a subject on which, apart from Circular 10/65 itself, there has been no Ministerial statement for a year. It is a subject which arouses intense discussion, and now absorbs much time and effort on the part of local education authorities. I think it only right, therefore, to try and put the basic issue in perspective, and to report to you on the progress so far made.

In doing so, I must warn you that I shall talk also about social and even political values. A few people still think that social and political aspirations can, and should, somehow be kept out of education. But of course they cannot and should not. Education and society interact on each other at every point. The structure of education must have a profound effect on the social structure—on the degree of equality, of equity, of opportunity, of social mobility; similarly, the content and character of education must profoundly influence the values and standards of adult society. Conversely, the social-class structure will affect the demand for education and the pool of ability available; likewise, the values and character of the society must affect what is taught in the schools and generally, indeed, the national attitude to education. And I hesitate to mention the further mundane but crucial fact that only elected politicians (and not, dare I say, even the wisest Royal Commission) can and should decide how much shall be spent on education as compared with other claims on our resources—

health, housing, pensions, roads, defence, or personal consumption.

It is for these reasons (obvious enough in all conscience) that in every society decisions about education—about priorities in spending or the organization of the school system—must have a social dimension and reflect value-judgments about justice, class, equality, ethics, or economic growth. It is for this reason that every educational philosophy, from Plato through Arnold to Dewey, has articulated the social and moral values of its time and of its author. And it is for this reason that every educational system in recorded history—whether of Athens or Sparta, of New Guinea or the Pueblo Indians, of Russia or America today—has mirrored the needs and aspirations of the community which created it. And as these needs and aspirations change, so the system must be changed if dangerous tensions are to be avoided.

It is against this background that we must see the movement towards comprehensive education. For I believe this represents a strong and irresistible pressure in British society to extend the rights of citizenship. Over the past three hundred years these rights have been extended first to personal liberty, then to political democracy, and later to social welfare. Now they must be further extended to educational equality. For until recently our schools have been essentially middle-class institutions, and our educational system essentially geared to educating the middle class, plus a few from below who aspired to be middle class or looked like desirable recruits to the middle class. The remainder were given cheaper teachers and inferior buildings and were segregated in separate schools. But today the pressure of democracy, under either political party, insists on full civil rights and full incorporation in the educational as in other fields.

However, let me now try to make the more specific case for comprehensive education and against the tripartite or bipartite system of schools which we have had since 1944. In summary, I believe this sytem to be educationally and socially unjust, inefficient, wasteful and divisive. I doubt if any indictment could be more wide-ranging than that.

First, and to me most important, I assert that separatism is socially unjust. Now to demonstrate this, I must ask you to consider what it is that we are measuring when, at 11-plus, (and however careful our selection procedures) we get out our labels and ticket our children, or most of them, for life: when, in Sir Frederick Clarke's phrase, we divide them up between the unselected goats and the carefully selected sheep.

Fifty years ago everyone, and even twenty years ago most people, would have answered that we were testing something, whether we called it measured intelligence, ability or aptitude, which was biologically inherited and fixed in a child for life. That was the philosophy which underlay the Hadow and Norwood Reports and the 1944 Act—that we were faced with children who differed from each other genetically and permanently, and who therefore needed to be educated in separate schools. By a further divine dispensation, fortunate indeed for the educational administrator, the differences fell into a precise numerical pattern—25 per cent academic and 75 per cent non-academic—which most conveniently fitted the existing pattern of schools.

Today we see matters quite differently. The researches of sociology and psychology have taught us, what only a few pioneers like Burt proclaimed in the past, that measured intelligence, unlike specific gravity, is not a fixed and innate quantity. It is not something given in limited measure in the genetic make-up of the new-born child. What is given is a bundle of assorted potentials, and what happens to them is a matter of nurture, of stimulus and response. The intelligence quotient is a function partly, of course, of inheritance, but also of environment and background.

Moreover, the environmental factors which exert the strongest influence on measured intelligence and hence on

educational performance—the factors of home and neighbourhood, of size of family and parental aspirations—are all strongly
linked to social class.

The first clear demonstration of this link between measured
performance and social class came within ten years of the
passage of the 1944 Act. The 'Early Leaving' report of the
Central Advisory Council in 1955 concluded, on the basis
of careful statistical research, that by the time of the 11-plus
examination, the children of certain social groups had begun
scholastically to outstrip those at the other end of the social
scale.[1] It further concluded that the improvement between
eleven and sixteen, which raised many pupils from the bottom
selection-group to the highest academic categories, was also
most common among those from professional and managerial
occupations. 'The boy', said the Central Advisory Council,
'whose father is of professional or managerial standing is more
likely to find his home circumstances favourable to the demands
of grammar school work than one whose father is an unskilled
or semi-skilled worker.' Thus it appeared that, quite apart from
any hereditary differences, the working-class boy suffered under
a clear social handicap; and that what we were testing by
examinations was perhaps as much home background as innate
intelligence.

I have mentioned this official inquiry, carried out for the
Central Advisory Council twelve years ago, because it demon-
strates that the challenge to the existing structure came quite
early on from the heart of the system. Two years later the
Floud and Halsey work *Social Class and Educational Opportunity*
was published,[2] a year later the British Psychological Society
inquiry, edited by Philip Vernon, on secondary school selection,[3] in 1963 the immense analyses in the Robbins appendix
by Professor Moser and the Ministry of Education statisticians,
measuring the pool of unused ability,[4] and in 1964 Dr Douglas's
work *The Home and the School*.[5] All this has reinforced the view
that I.Q. and educational performance are heavily influenced
by environment as well as by heredity, and that many working-

class children suffer a pronounced environmental handicap as compared with middle-class children of the same ability.

What then are we doing when, at the age of eleven, we divide our children into 25 per cent grammar and 75 per cent secondary modern? It is not, I suppose, in dispute that the grammar school offers more in terms of life-chances. The grammar school child—and I am talking now of children of the same level of attainment and the same potential when they start at secondary school—has a statistically much greater chance than the secondary modern child of going on to higher education, and of commanding, therefore, a wide choice of occupations. He is four or five times as likely to be prepared by subject specialists for the examinations which lead to higher education. He will generally be taught in smaller classes: the pupil-teacher ratio in January 1964 was 17·5, compared with 20·3 in the secondary modern schools. The latest salary analysis shows that over 70 per cent of grammar school staff are paid salaries above the basic scale, compared with 45 per cent in secondary modern schools. John Vaizey suggested in 1958 that the average grammar school child received 170 per cent more a year in terms of resources than the average secondary modern school child; and there is no reason to think that the differential has been narrowed since then.

This is in no way to minimize the remarkable efforts of the secondary modern schools in recent years. It is to their enormous credit that without the stimulus of the top 20 per cent of ability they have nevertheless helped able youngsters to get good G.C.E. results and to go on to higher education. But this has been in spite of the odds being loaded against them. Given, then, that the grammar school offers more ample chances and opportunities in after-life, and given that I.Q. at eleven reflects home background as well as innate intelligence, what the 11-plus is doing is this: it penalizes the working-class boy not necessarily for innate stupidity but partly for his social background, for his less educated parents, his larger family, his crowded home, his slum neighbourhood, his generally less favourable environment. And at the same time we diminish his opportunities for improving his ability by continued education. Already in the eighteenth century no less an authority than Dr Johnson said, 'I do not deny, Sir, but there is some original difference in minds; but it is nothing in comparison of what is formed by education.' Now in the twentieth century, research has confirmed that measured ability is a function, not only of heredity and environment, but also of the educational process itself. Whatever may be the endowment at birth, and however social environment may smile or frown upon it, good schooling will make more of it than poor schooling, and longer schooling will take it further than schooling cut short. This influence of educational stimulation on intelligence grows more profound with age, and may well be decisive in the years from fifteen to twenty. Yet we deny the opportunity for this stimulus to large sections of our population because of their social background at the age of eleven.

Thus, we punish the working-class boy for his social origins not once but in a series of successive stages. For under the present system, with streaming in primary schools followed by selection at 11-plus, the working-class child of similar abilities to the middle-class child at the age of eight does progressively worse at the primary school, has less chance of obtaining a grammar school place, and falls still further behind from eleven onwards.

Now of course we cannot wholly correct an unfavourable background by a change in school organization. The argument goes far wider than educational policy. To make equal opportunity in education a reality, we shall have not only to eliminate bad housing and inadequate incomes, but steadily to make good the educational deficiencies of parents who cannot give their children the encouragement they need. True equality of opportunity cannot be accomplished in one generation, or by education alone; it needs a wider social revolution.

But as soon as we concede that measured intelligence is not a quantity fixed for life, and that it depends, moreover, partly on the child's environment, we must surely think it indefensible to segregate children into different schools at the age of eleven. It is, of course, in the nature of things that as we grow to manhood we go different ways. Life itself is a selective process. But we must allow that process to work fairly; we must allow time for the beneficial influence of education to compensate for the deficiencies of upbringing and early circumstance. Segregation as early as 11-plus is indefensible. We must keep the choices open, and defer as long as possible the irrevocable selection. Amid all the shifting contours of educational planning I am certain of this: that the system must allow the individual to pick up, to make good, to try again. You do not feed a child less because it grows slowly or has some initial handicap to overcome.

To me, then, the central and irresistible argument against the 11-plus lies in the denial of social justice and equal opportunity which it implies. And as though this denial were not enough, we superimpose on it, as you all well know, a further geographical inequity. I refer to the notorious fact that, in what passes for a national system of education, there are thirteen authorities providing selected places for less than 15 per cent of pupils, and twenty-nine authorities providing for over 25 per cent—and one of them almost 40 per cent. These facts alone would impel us to change, not for the sake of administrative tidiness, but for the sake of the youngsters, whose life-chances are so arbitrarily determined according to where they happen to be born.

However, perhaps arguments based on social justice will seem too remote to hard-headed educational administrators—though I have never noticed, happily, that such people in England are lacking in principle or idealism; far from it. But lest we still have left a nucleus of conscienceless bureaucrats, I turn now to my second argument against separatism. This is based on the inefficiency implicit in it. I refer especially to the extreme fallibility, the hit-and-miss nature, of the process of selection. Wherever you draw the line, there will be people on either side of it with very little between them, quite apart from the fact that from one test to another a child's I.Q. performance can and does vary considerably.

In the early 'fifties, as you know, intensive research was carried out which showed that while the procedures applied by local authorities—using standardized tests and teachers' assessments—were in one sense highly efficient, there were still about 10–12 per cent of 'wrong' allocations made each year. That is to say, for every hundred children, some five or six were allocated to secondary modern schools who, had they been sent to grammar schools, might have been more successful than another five or six who were in fact sent to grammar school. And if we allow for the fact that children actually allocated to grammar schools would be expected to show up better than those who were not, the results suggest that the number of really 'wrong' allocations may have been much larger. I may add that subsequent transfers enabled only one or two children per hundred to move into grammar schools from secondary modern. This shows the acute danger of miscalculation at the age of eleven; it also shows how hard it is to correct the miscalculation if you segregate children into different schools.

But there is also—and this is my third argument—a wider social waste involved. If ever there was a country which needed to make the most of its resources, it is Britain in the second half of the twentieth century; and the chief resource of a crowded island is its people. Moreover, the proportion of relatively inexpert and unskilled jobs to be done declines from year to year. To behave in these circumstances as though there were a fixed 25 per cent of top ability at eleven not only flies in the face of the evidence which I have quoted; it amounts to feckless prodigality.

The extent to which we are wasting good educational talent, for what are in part social causes, was fully and horrifyingly documented in the Crowther and Robbins Reports. Not all the waste, of course, is linked with the 11-plus; some is due to early leaving or poor performance in grammar school. Yet it is also clear that, despite all that has been done in the secondary modern schools by able and devoted teachers to minimize the damage, there has been a frightful waste of latent talent through the sheer fact of segregation, through the discouragement put upon a large group of the population by the label of failure. The proof lies in the subsequent upgrading in comprehensive schools of the 11-plus failures, and indeed in the award of some of our highest academic honours to those who at eleven had fallen on the wrong side of the line.

There are, I believe, two ways in which a fully comprehensive system will minimize this waste. One relates to the element of self-fulfilling prophecy in the educational system. We know from researches how vital are the expectations of parents and teachers to the performance of the children. Children expected to do well, on the whole, do well; children marked with the brand of failure on the whole will fail.

Failure in the 11-plus—the only exam, as has recently been pointed out, in which three-quarters of those concerned know they must fail—is conspicuously such a brand. If anyone doubts this they have only to see the effect of failing the 11-plus on the morale of both parents and children.

But if, by eliminating early selection, we could also lessen the early sense of failure, we might not only avoid a lot of unnecessary human misery; we might also find a sharp increase in the performance of many of the 75 per cent who now so often fulfil the gloomy prophecy made about them at the cruelly early age of eleven.

In addition, the truly comprehensive school is given an enormous impetus and inspiration by having within it the full range of ability. The secondary modern schools have, to their credit, introduced G.C.E. courses for the benefit of those who could profit by them; but without the example of the top range of ability as pace-setters, it is all too easy for children not to make the effort, to accept society's verdict and let it go at that.

For we all know how much students learn informally rather

than formally, from each other rather than from their elders. We know that standards in a school are partly set by what sociologists call 'the student culture', by the young taste-makers and opinion-moulders. If these are hostile to brains, hostile to school and the teacher, then intellectual standards will be low. But to the extent that an academic stream exists, setting at least one model and acting as intellectual pacemaker, to that extent the standard will improve. It must, surely, be the experience of many of you here, as it is the finding of studies on both sides of the Atlantic, that the achievement of those who would otherwise be in a secondary modern school, and notably those in the middle ranges of ability, where the greatest waste is now, is markedly higher in a comprehensive school—due to the extra stimulus, the fizz (in Mr Mason's graphic phrase), the upgrading imparted by the academic stream

But what of the bright boy? Will he not suffer? And, more generally, is not an elitist system, a Platonic meritocracy, essential to efficiency and survival in a competitive and scientific world? As to the latter point, I have little anxiety. We have long combined almost the most elitist educational system with almost the slowest rate of economic growth of any advanced industrial nation. Both America and Sweden with their comprehensive systems have outstripped us in efficiency. I should suppose that what we most need from this point of view is a huge widening of educational opportunity. There is no evidence at all that we need to preserve selection at 11-plus.

And why should the bright boy or girl suffer by attending a comprehensive rather than a selective grammar school? Exact comparison is difficult in Britain, because most comprehensive schools operate in areas where the grammar schools still cream off a large proportion of the brighter pupils. But there is some evidence, from a large-scale international research project not yet published, that in mathematics, at least, the bright pre-university pupils in countries with a comprehensive system do just as well as similar pupils in countries with a highly selective system such as our own. Moreover, to support the point which I have just made, the mathematics performance of pupils of lower ability is much higher in the comprehensive countries than in selective countries. This would suggest both that 'more' does not necessarily mean 'worse' for brighter pupils, and that the total 'yield' may be greater in a comprehensive system.

In Britain, indeed, the comprehensive schools may be so concerned to do as well academically as the grammar schools that the danger may be the opposite one—too much concentration on the bright pupils. But this danger will no doubt be counteracted as the need to compete narrowly with the grammar schools disappears.

A particular fear is also expressed, which one must again respect, that the grammar or direct grant schools provide the only opportunity for bright working-class boys to rise out of their class and obtain an academic education. I think the point I have just made largely answers this. And there is this further point. One must not disregard the wastage of working-class children which already occurs from the grammar schools, where they are much less likely than boys from better homes —even when they have gained admission—to stay on and do well. This may be bound up with one of the weaknesses which the grammar schools have developed under the selective system—namely, a comparative neglect (sometimes an almost callous neglect) of their lower streams who are thought not to be up to the G.C.E.

I pass now from social waste to my fourth argument—a more controversial one, though I personally feel it deeply: that separate schools exacerbate social division. It cannot be denied that the 11-plus divides overwhelmingly according to social class: indeed, because of streaming in the primary school, social-class division in schools begins to operate at the age of eight. What we euphemistically describe as educational selection is for the most part social selection; and our educational division is largely a class division.

This is so partly for the perhaps natural reason that schools

and teachers react to social as well as to educational factors. As
Dr Douglas reminds us, 'Children who come from well-kept
homes and who are themselves clean, well clothed and shod,
stand a greater chance of being put in the upper streams than
their measured ability would seem to justify.' But of course the
more fundamental cause is the one which I have already
stressed: that measured intelligence at eleven is partly a function
of environment, and that environment is closely linked with
social class. What we are testing at eleven, therefore, is to a
large extent social-class background.

Now by selecting for a superior school children who are
already well-favoured by environment, we are not merely
confirming, we are hardening and sharpening, an existing
social division. This can surely not be thought desirable. I will
not argue the point in terms of equality. But I will argue it in
terms of a sense of community, of social cohesion, of a nation
composed of people who understand each other because they
can communicate. If the only time we can, as a society, achieve
this common language is when we go to war, then we are at a
much less advanced stage than many societies which the
anthropologists describe as primitive. We have only to consider
our industrial relations, and the lack of communication and
mutual understanding reflected in them, to see the depth of
social division in Britain today. Of course, education alone
cannot solve this problem. But so long as we choose to educate
our children in separate camps, reinforcing and seeming to
validate existing differences in accent, language and values, for
so long will our schools exacerbate rather than diminish our
class divisions.

Of course the elimination of separatism at 11-plus is only a
necessary, and not a sufficient, condition of reducing the
divisive effect of our school system. We should not much improve matters if selection gave way merely to rigid streaming
within a strictly neighbourhood pattern of schools. This
would re-create many of the old evils within a comprehensive
system.

When I speak of streaming, I naturally do not mean to imply that it can, or should be avoided, totally and at every age. I refer to unnecessarily early and rigid streaming. Here of course there must be an improvement as a result of comprehensive reorganization, and in the place that matters most—the primary schools. We all know what strains and rigidities the 11-plus has imposed on the primary schools—the over-emphasis on tracking and streaming and cramming. But the case for early streaming will disappear as the 11-plus disappears. There will, indeed, be much wider scope in the primary schools for innovation and experiment and the release of creative ability—from teachers and pupils alike. The newer and better methods of teaching, in mathematics, in English and in French, are more likely to be tried and more likely to bring good results; and subjects like music are less likely to get crowded out of the curriculum.

And as far as the comprehensives themselves are concerned, I am most interested, as I go round the country, to find how strong is the reaction against some of the early practices of rigid and premature streaming. There seems to be a general loosening-up and a greater willingness to experiment.

The problem of the one-class neighbourhood school is more intractable. It is not, of course, a problem created by going comprehensive: four out of five secondary modern schools are neighbourhood schools, and most grammar and direct grant schools are predominantly middle class—they do not become classless merely by having a small working-class stratum, any more than the House of Commons became truly representative of British society sixty years ago merely because Keir Hardie was elected to it. The problem is the result of gross social inequality combined with bad town-planning. In the long term the mere fact of wider educational opportunity will gradually improve matters. In the short term it is for the local authorities to give close attention to the boundaries of catchment areas; and in Circular 10/65 I have urged them to make such schools as socially and intellectually comprehensive as is practicable, perhaps by linking together two districts of a different character. This is very much the kind of problem on which further light will, I hope, be thrown by the special programme of research that the Government has launched.

Even with rigid streaming and neighbourhood schools, it would be hard to maintain that a comprehensive system could produce as sharp a social cleavage as the present division into separate schools. But with the elimination of streaming in primary schools, the movement against premature streaming in the comprehensive schools, and the growing realization by local education authorities of the need to make their new comprehensives socially heterogeneous, I think I may reasonably claim that the new system will reduce the sense of social division and increase the sense of social cohesion in contemporary British society.

It was, I think, these various considerations—of equity, efficiency, avoidance of waste and social cohesion—which produced over the last decade an increasing revulsion against the 11-plus, and a gathering movement towards comprehensives. And it was they which caused this Government to set the seal of national approval on this movement by the issue of Circular 10/65.

There were, of course, those who urged us not to act—in particular, the melancholy waiters; 'wait for Plowden', 'wait for research', wait for something or other. Of course they were too late. Whatever the Government did or did not do, reorganization schemes were being prepared at local level; it was surely not proposed that the Government should veto them all when they arrived in Curzon Street.

'Waiting for Plowden' was in any case an impractical suggestion. The Council is not due to report until this summer. Any proposal for an altered age of transfer would arouse, I imagine, strong controversy throughout the educational world. The Government would have to allow an ample period for argument, debate and consultation with all the interests concerned. At the end of this period, any decision to change the national age of transfer would require the lengthy process of a new Education Act. We are surely talking here in years, not months. I could not allow hundreds of thousands of children to suffer the injustice and fallibility of the 11-plus for this long period.

Again, it is said that the Government should have awaited the results of research. This is not a suggestion which I will accept from my political opponents. For no previous educational change—including the 1944 Act—ever waited on the results of research; nor, if it comes to that, did previous Ministers, when they approved many comprehensive schools and schemes.

But I would not criticize them for this, because the 'waiting for research' argument betrays a misunderstanding of the nature both of educational research and of our political system. Educational research, in any case a very new tool, can give new facts, illuminate the range of choice, show how better to achieve a given objective, but it cannot say what the objective ought to be. For this must depend, as I tried to make clear earlier, on judgments which have a value-component and a social dimension—judgments about equity and equal opportunity and social division and economic efficiency and all the other criteria which I have mentioned in this speech. These judgments cannot be made in the National Foundation for Educational Research. They can be made only in Parliament and the local Council chamber.

The purpose of research is quite different. It is, by fact-finding surveys and evaluative studies, to help local authorities, and their administrators and teachers, to carry out this major reform more effectively. I delight in the fact, that for the first time in our educational history, such studies will be built into a major reform from the outset. We owe it to those who will be running the education service, and teaching in its schools, a generation hence, that we make proper provision now for informed policy-making in the years to come. But it can be no substitute for taking those decisions in our own generation which must be taken, in common fairness, to give those children now in the schools the best opportunity we can to advance themselves and their society. Those decisions are a part of the political process; there is nowhere to take them for settlement except into the political arena.

I conclude with a brief progress report. Of course the Government never supposed that by declaring our objective we made its achievement quick or simple. We knew that we faced some inescapable physical facts which must limit the speed of change; and we were determined, moreover, to build the new systems on the foundations of what was best in the old. You cannot wind up one educational system at the end of the summer term and start a new one the following September. What is important is that we should move as quickly as we can but as slowly as we must. I count progress not on a score-sheet of how many authorities claim to abolish the 11-plus, but of how many authorities provide genuine comprehensive education. It is easy enough to do the first without doing the second. But the essence of the operation is not to deprive the selected minority of children of a good education, but to give something better to all children.

I have referred to inescapable physical facts. You will be even more conscious of these than I am. We have about 6,000 secondary schools, nearly half in post-war buildings. The overwhelming majority, new buildings as well as old, were designed for a separatist system. Few are large enough to be transformed easily into orthodox all-through comprehensive schools. Often, therefore, we must resort to forms of organization which divide children horizontally by age, instead of vertically by ability; that is, to various forms of two-tier system. I do not want to see any of these last for ever, where they involve the creation of two-year schools, whether the two years are eleven to thirteen or fourteen to sixteen. But I could not rule them out altogether. Nor can I rule out the device of using separate sets of buildings for a single school. To do so would have been to put the Government's policy into a deep freeze for many years to come.

So we must make the best progress we can with our existing stock of buildings. I hope I have made it clear beyond question, both in Circular 10/65 and in some of my decisions on individual plans, that I do not intend to agree to any arrangements which result simply in children and teachers being distributed between a given set of buildings so that they all have roofs over their heads, but nobody has a real school. I do not want sham comprehensives. But I am profoundly pleased to see how many authorities, despite a shortage both of time and money, have found, or are finding, constructive and imaginative ways of moving towards a truly comprehensive pattern. Many authorities, particularly in the north, were of course well on with the preparation of reorganization plans some years ago; for them, Circular 10/65 was merely the central government following the lead of local government. But I am most impressed by the way in which authorities who have started from the Circular have set about what I know is the really tremendous task of producing plans by next July.

In this connection I want to say something about the direct grant schools. In recent months I have mentioned them specifically in two distinct but related contexts: Circular 10/65, and the anouncement of the Public Schools Commission. In the Circular I urged local education authorities and the governors of the schools to find ways, in the schemes of comprehensive organization called for by the Circular, of continuing and developing their tradition of co-operation. Naturally, therefore, when I announced the Public Schools Commission, I said that its terms of reference did not include the direct grant schools. To have brought them within the ambit of the Commission would have caused total confusion. We must have one policy, not two, for the direct grant sector; and the one policy is laid down in Circular 10/65.

I have heard it suggested that the direct grant regulations prevent the schools from negotiating with local education authorities in accordance with the Circular on the grounds that regulation 17 requires them to be academically selective;

o

this, it is said, is inconsistent with their participating in comprehensive schemes. I want to make it clear that I do not, repeat not, regard the regulations as a genuine obstacle to co-operation in schemes of secondary reorganization. The only obligation which could possibly be construed as requiring a school to be selective is to be found in the concluding words of regulation 17 (1); and this is expressly subject to any arrangements which the school makes with the authority. If, however, there is any real doubt on this subject, I shall not hesitate to amend the regulations in a way which would leave no room for any doubt at all.

In the Circular, and in my Parliamentary statement about the Public Schools Commission, I have twice expressed my hope that the direct grant schools and the local education authorities will find ways of co-operation within a system of comprehensive education. This is still my hope. If events prove me wrong, then the whole future of the direct grant system will inevitably come into question.

Speaking of co-operation, let me emphasize once again that comprehensive reform must be carried through in close co-operation with the teachers. Any educational system must have the support of teachers, since only teachers can make schools work. It follows that consultation between authorities and teachers is not just a formal stage in the process of producing a plan—it is absolutely vital. As I come to consider individual plans I shall pay special attention to this point, and shall want to be satisfied that ample time has been allowed for teachers to make their proper contribution.

Any new organization must give the majority of children more opportunities than did the old. I believe that the old social and intellectual stratification of the school system is no longer acceptable to democratic opinion in the 1960s. We must therefore set ourselves a new objective, which is not to deprive the minority of their present educational standards, but to give all our children a more ample opportunity.

17 *Pluralism in Higher Education*

Speech delivered at the University of Lancaster on
January 20th, 1967

I must begin by mentioning a severely practical reason for this
policy and the system of higher education that goes with it.
That is that the system already existed. The present Government did not invent it; it had been developing steadily since the
turn of the century or earlier. Alongside the universities there
were the training colleges under local authority or denomi-
national control; and there was a strong and growing sector of
higher education in Further Education. Indeed Table 3 of the
Robbins Report[1] showed, perhaps to the surprise of many
people, that over 40 per cent of students in full-time higher education were outside the universities.

This was the plural or binary system—whatever you choose
to call it—which we inherited. Were we then to convert it into
a unitary system entirely under university control? I do not
know whether this was seriously suggested. True, we differed
from Robbins about the colleges of education; I shall refer to
this later. But as far as Further Education is concerned, while
there may have been argument about the future of a tiny number of colleges, it could hardly be proposed that it should
altogether lose its higher education sector. Certainly the Robbins Committee never proposed this; indeed the whole
rationale of their proposal for the Council for National Academic Awards (C.N.A.A.) was precisely to strengthen this
sector.

The plain fact is that we did not start off *tabula rasa*; we
started off with a given historical situation. A plural system

already existed; and whatever anyone's views as to how they might have liked to start off from scratch, we could not, two years ago, have done a major surgical operation and converted the existing system into an entirely different one. We could not, for example, have taken the 35,000 full-time and sandwich students doing higher education in Further Education, or even the 9,000 degree and Dip. Tech. students, and transferred them to the universities; apart from anything else, this would have split all the leading colleges right down the middle. It would have been utterly wrong, at a time of rapid expansion in higher education, if all the various authorities—autonomous universities, local education authorities, voluntary bodies, boards of governors—had been thrown into a melting-pot of administrative reform, merely for the sake of tidiness.

So much for the severely practical reason. But there were also, in the Government's view, strong arguments on merit for maintaining the plural system which we inherited. One such argument relates to social control. I expressed this badly at Woolwich,[2] because I could have been understood to imply that the universities were not socially responsive. Of course I did not intend to imply any such thing. I would not suggest for a moment that they are not responsive to any intimation of the national need that they can discern for themselves, or that Governments are able to give them. They always have been responsive and never more so than today. Yet given the high degree of autonomy which they enjoy, there is a sense in which the other colleges can be said to be under more direct social control. This becomes clear if one considers (to take one or two rather extreme examples) the 20 per cent productivity exercise in the colleges of education, or the control over courses and class-sizes in the technical colleges. And I would add two wider points; firstly, that it is in my view a valuable feature of our democratic tradition that elected representatives and local authorities should maintain a stake in higher education; secondly, that at a time of rapid expansion and changing ideas, what is wanted is not a monopoly situation in higher education, but a variety of institutions under different control—a unitary system would surely imply an omniscience which we do not possess.

No doubt the distinction between the universities and other colleges will lessen, as on the one hand we seek to give more academic freedom to the latter, and on the other hand, the universities come under growing, though friendly, scrutiny from the University Grants Committee and public and Parliamentary opinion. But I feel clear that side by side with an autonomous sector of higher education there must also be a public or social sector.

I now turn to certain particular arguments which influenced the Government's policy. I take first the colleges of education. The question of their control was one of the very small number of the 178 recommendations of the Robbins Committee that the Government did not see its way to accepting.

We decided, contrary to Robbins, that the colleges should continue to be administered by their present sponsors. We took this view for a number of reasons. We thought it unwise to change horses in the middle of a turbulent period of expansion, especially at a moment when the universities themselves were also in the middle of very rapid change and development. We had faith in the readiness of the local authorities and the voluntary bodies to make such liberal changes in the government of the colleges as their growing status required. And we saw no sufficient reason to divorce the colleges from the public and voluntary bodies, which had brought them into existence to serve a specific and urgent social need, namely, to provide the schools with well-qualified teachers.

In passing I must say again, as I have often said before, how much we all owe to the colleges for the way in which they have responded to the social need by their readiness to absorb a large increase in students and also, and very important, by their readiness to consider more productive patterns of organization.

Now this policy of preserving the existing administration in the colleges was subject to two riders. One was that the Government would encourage universities to open up degree opportunities for suitably qualified students of the colleges, and the other was that the local authorities and voluntary bodies should take such steps as were needed to liberalize the government of the colleges. We have not been disappointed on either count. On the first point, the universities, with the one exception of Cambridge, have been energetic in tackling the job of tailoring their degree requirements to suit the special needs of the colleges, and I am grateful to them for their co-operation in this. As far as the government of the colleges is concerned, a working group of local education authorities, the voluntary bodies and the colleges themselves, under the able chairmanship of Mr Weaver, drew up a statement of the principles by which they thought the colleges should be governed. I think that those of you who have read the report of the study group would agree that it is marked by a co-operative spirit as well as by a good deal of administrative precision. And personally I share the view of the university representatives, who helped us in this work that if we can carry out these recommendations, the colleges will have a greatly increased responsibility for their academic work and greater freedom to perform it. I am determined to see that the recommendations are carried out. The Government are prepared to introduce the legislation which the study group thought necessary, and I intend shortly to issue a circular inviting all concerned to act on the report's recommendations.

I turn now to the Further Education sector, with particular reference to the Polytechnics. I need not rehearse the various general arguments—educational, social and economic—for maintaining a strong, though distinctive, higher education element in Further Education, if only because the Robbins Report itself so readily conceded the case.

But I want to refer to one argument of great immediacy. There are two categories of students whose importance to the nation can hardly be overestimated. Firstly, there are the tens of thousands of students who want to do a full-time course which, although not of degree standard, leads to one or other of the many professional qualifications marked by a certificate or an associateship. Secondly, there is the huge and growing army of part-time students at all levels, almost all of them already in employment. Now the universities cannot cater for these without a complete transformation of the university system, of a kind which would not be practicable for many years ahead, and which, in any case, neither Robbins nor anyone else has recommended. We must therefore cater for them in the technical colleges and in the future Polytechnics.

But is it not then highly desirable that these colleges should also embrace a third category of full-time degree students? Firstly, there are strong educational arguments for this. I believe that there will be great educational advantage from the existence, alongside the universities, of more broadly based higher education institutions, in which full-time, sandwich and part-time students, at all levels of higher education, work together. In academic as well as human terms, there is no hard and fast line between the different categories. Each will have much to gain, and much to give, and all will benefit from belonging to the same academic community.

Secondly, the inclusion of full-time degree work carries on the historic and invaluable Further Education tradition of providing opportunities for educational and social mobility. The colleges have always catered, amongst others, for the students who cannot, on entry, show that they are of university calibre, and for those who can profit from a university course, but cannot give their whole time to it. Technical college teachers could quote hundreds of examples of students in these categories who have been helped by good teaching and their own strong motivation subsequently to tackle a full-time degree course. Perhaps they left school early, perhaps they were late developers, perhaps they were first-generation aspirants to higher education, who were too modest at the right moment to apply to a university, perhaps they had started on a career and thought that a technical college course would more directly improve their qualifications for doing it. The important thing is that the leading technical colleges, by their capacity to provide for students at different levels of ability and attainment (and that is why I call them comprehensive), provide a chance for students of these kinds not only to tackle degree-level work part-time or full-time, but also to develop their latent capacity to do so. This range of opportunity is a precious part of this country's educational heritage that we would be mad to abandon. No wonder some other countries envy what has come to be called the open-ended role of the technical colleges—the role of providing the second chance, the alternative route.

Thirdly, the inclusion of full-time degree work is the best way of avoiding a most undesirable social and educational division at eighteen. It is sometimes said by critics of the Government's policy that, just as we are abolishing the 11+, we are creating a new 18+. Now I am very dubious about analogies between these two ages. At 11+, an entire age-group is moving up and it can do so either selectively or non-selectively; but at 18+, whatever the system of higher education, there must be some selection because only a proportion of the age-group goes into higher education at all. It therefore seems hard to draw any useful analogy from the one situation to the other.

However, if one is talking generally of educational divisions at eighteen, the present system is surely infinitely preferable to that implied in the criticisms of my Woolwich speech. The critics see, of course, the need for the Further Education sector. But the implication of their criticism is that we should give the universities a virtual monopoly of degree-level work, either by eliminating it from Further Education or by transferring some Further Education institutions to the university sector. In other words, they want to cream off most, if not all, full-time degree work into the universities, leaving the Further Education sector to sub-degree and part-time work. This would not only run counter to the whole British tradition and indeed to the

Robbins Report. It would truly be 'binary' with a vengeance, converting the technical colleges into upper-level secondary modern schools and dividing the eighteen-year-olds into a privileged university class of full-time degree students with the remainder in Further Education. I can imagine nothing more socially or educationally divisive.

These are the reasons why we see the Polytechnics as comprehensive in their student intake, embracing full-time work, as well as the two categories I mentioned earlier. As to the Polytechnics, I think their creation has been generally welcomed, although there are two conflicting criticisms that have been made. It is said that we are preserving a privileged position for the universities by deliberately trying to create inferior institutions outside. This is contradicted by the equally unfounded fear that we are trying to raise a phalanx of state universities, which will fulfil the same function as the existing universities. I do not think anybody who reads the White Paper on Polytechnics could say that there is anything in it to justify either of these two mutually inconsistent criticisms. What we see as the role of the Polytechnics is something distinctive from the universities, and more comprehensive in the way I indicated earlier.

When we say that the polytechnics will be primarily teaching institutions, of course we do not wish to deny the staff opportunities for research, to serve the needs of local industry, or to enlarge their knowledge and understanding of their own disciplines. Again, to say that the degrees awarded by C.N.A.A. will be comparable in standard to university degrees is not to say, very much the opposite, that in content and treatment their courses should be a slavish copy of university courses. I hope they certainly will not be that. In terms of the type of degree and the balance between teaching and research, as well as the comprehensive character of the student intake, we see the Polytechnics as fulfilling a distinctive role from the universities.

Finally, I want to allay one anxiety which has been aroused

by our policy, and that is that the dividing line between the two sectors might be too rigid. This is the last thing we want. The fact is that the work and functions of the two sectors are not mutually exclusive. There is, and should be, a great deal of variety and a great deal of overlap.

Thus we want to encourage mutual co-operation between institutions in the two sectors, while each preserves its own identity. We want to encourage exchange of staff, exchange of students, students of one place going to lectures at another, the joint use of student facilities, the shared use of expensive equipment, and particularly at post-graduate level a high degree of mutual co-operation. The colleges of education already look to the universities for the B.Ed., and there are five leading technical colleges starting up departments of education in co-operation with university institutes. We shall, I am sure, increasingly want to encourage collaboration on a regional basis to ensure that costly resources are used in the most rational manner.

We also want to work towards the equalization of standards of amenity for students between the different sectors, wherever this is appropriate. We have, over a great part of the field, a common system of student awards; and we shall work towards making it still more comprehensive. We have produced common building standards for student residence in all sectors of higher education, which means that where neighbouring institutions of different types want to create a common residential area, as I hope they will, they will not encounter difficulties in the shape of different cost limits. We are working towards the same objective in other kinds of higher education building. We have worked, in the Weaver Report,[3] towards the liberalization of the government of the Colleges of Education, and we shall do the same thing with the leading technical colleges.

I hope I have said enough to make it clear that we do not want any rigid dividing line between the different sectors— quite the contrary. I think these fears partly arose because 'binary' is possibly not the best word to describe the system of higher education in this country, and you will notice that I have tried to avoid it. If one compares our system with that in other countries, one finds we have a strikingly varied, plural and diverse system—universities, colleges of education, polytechnics, colleges of further education, and a large variety of monotechnic institutions of one kind and another. I think this variety and diversity is thoroughly healthy, and we should seek to preserve it.

18 *Resources for Education*

Address to the annual general meeting of the Association of Education Committees, at Brighton, on June 23rd, 1967.

In recent years we have heard a fundamental criticism, and made from more than one quarter, that we are trying to do too much with limited resources. It has been argued that we cannot accomplish all our policies—raising the leaving-age, reorganizing secondary education, doing more for the primary schools, expanding higher education, and so on—with the resources likely to be available to us. We cannot, as the phrase goes, get a quart out of a pint pot; and we therefore should, to change the metaphor, cut our coat according to our cloth, and give up some of our ambitions.

This is an important criticism, which one must respect—and not only for the reason that it has been made by your secretary (though that is a powerful enough reason in itself). It is a criticism which shows a down-to-earth approach to questions of educational advance, and to that extent is a great improvement on some of the rather starry-eyed claims that were being made, only a few years back, by well-meaning enthusiasts in all parts of the education service and outside it. I greatly welcome the fact that the question of available resources, and the consequential question of priorities, is now being actively discussed. Your president, when he spoke to you on Wednesday, put some of the arguments before you with great force. With much of what Alderman Hutty said I fully agree, though I would like, if I may, to put the emphasis rather differently in one or two respects.

In particular, I would like to inject into the discussion two considerations which are sometimes forgotten. The first is that we are not in fact dealing with a pint pot in the sense of operating within a fixed and unchanging total of resources. Alderman Hutty touched on this, and I would like to develop the point a little further. To begin with, the total of national resources grows from year to year, not, of course, as fast as one would like, but nevertheless appreciably over a period of years. At constant prices the national product last year was 16 per cent higher than five years previously, and 33 per cent higher than ten years previously. So the production of national wealth increased by a third in a decade.

Moreover, the share of education in the total is not fixed either. Of course we should expect education to obtain its proportionate share of this growing national income. But in fact, throughout this period, it has been taking a rising share of this rising total. Excluding meals and milk, spending on public education, as a proportion of national income, has risen over the last ten years from $3\frac{1}{2}$ to $5\frac{1}{2}$ per cent. This has meant an increase of $2\frac{1}{4}$ times, at constant prices, in the size of the resources put into education. So the resources at our disposal are very far from being fixed; they are expanding year by year.

My other thought is that the pressure on these resources—the pressure of educational demands and needs and commitments —does not grow continuously at a steady pace. Of course part of the pressure does—the demand for higher standards, for example; indeed it is the greatly increased public interest in education, and the more ambitious horizons which parents now have for their children, which provide the justification for a bigger share of resources being devoted to it. But other parts of the pressure on us have more of the aspect of an ebb and flow. For it is a fact about demographic change that while it sometimes adds to the strain on the country's resources, at other times it eases the strain. For example, the size of the eighteen-year-old age-group, after a period of rapid growth, is now on a plateau, and by 1970 will actually be 25 per cent smaller than it was in 1965. Or, again, the fall in the birthrate in the last two or three years will ease the position in the primary schools after 1970 when numbers in the secondary schools will be increasing.

So there is a growing national income, a growing share for education in it, and a constantly changing demographic picture which provide both the need and the opportunity to adjust our priorities as we go along. The share of any particular part of the service in the education budget is no more fixed than is the education budget, or the national income of which the education budget in turn is a part. The picture is more fluid, more encouraging, less static than the tinker's metaphor of the quart and the pint pot would suggest.

I mention these considerations only to put the argument of limited resources into perspective, not of course to deny that we are under great pressure to meet all the demands made on us. Although the historical perspective is perhaps more cheerful than some people realize, all of us here are only too conscious of how strong the immediate pressure is.

How should we react to it? First, of course, we must react by spending our money as wisely, as efficiently and as economically as we can, to ensure that we get the greatest possible value for it. We must increase the use of industrialized building till we approach the point where we achieve a definite saving in cost. We must exploit all the possibilities of shared and extended use of buildings and sports facilities. In higher education, we must encourage the present efforts towards a more intensive use of buildings and capital equipment and higher productivity generally.

Let me give one example of how we can organize our resources to get better value for money, an example which shows what can be achieved by central and local government working together. The furniture that goes into a building is almost as important as the building itself; unsuitable furniture can wholly spoil a well-designed building. Yet until recently, while much skill was applied to improving the design of school buildings, comparatively little was done to improve the design of school furniture. In the course of development projects carried out by our architects, ideas emerged for a range of school furniture which would be more in keeping with the modern educational trends which we are trying to encourage. But while we could exert some influence, we could not, unaided, make any considerable impact on the general standard of design.

The situation has now completely altered as a result of co-operation between my Department and two other organizations—the Ministry of Public Building and Works and the CLASP Consortium of local education authorities. The Ministry of Public Building and Works have great experience of large-scale procurement of furniture, and they contributed their expertise in translating basic designs into manufacturing specifications and in the letting of contracts. The CLASP Consortium has been crucial in guaranteeing a sufficient market to enable contracts of a worthwhile size to be placed with manufacturers. As a result, an increasing number of primary schools are receiving furniture from a complete range which is consistent in its dimensional basis and in its style and finish. I saw this furniture when it was displayed recently in London, and I can confirm that it is not only robust and functional, but attractive and well designed. I believe that where it is already in use teachers are delighted with it and with the greater flexibility which it gives them. We are now wishing to extend the range into the secondary field.

This is a good illustration of the sort of enterprise which the Government envisaged in its recent White Paper on *Public Purchasing and Industrial Efficiency*.[1] I hope to see it go ahead and expand still further. If it does, and if more authorities come in and make use of it, we shall be able to exploit the advantages of large orders and longer production runs, and so make prices even more competitive. We shall achieve better value for money as well as better design.

But however efficient and economical we are, we shall only diminish and not eliminate the problem of pressure on resources. We shall still not be able to do everything we want. We shall therefore still have consciously to choose priorities. Any Government (central or local) must do this, and must do it all the time; indeed this is a large part (some would say the decisive part) of the function and art of government.

In the past this process has been somewhat haphazard, characterized largely by expediency and empiricism. These have their part in government, as they have in every department of life, but they are not on their own a sufficient basis for taking government decisions; and it is a fundamental aspect of this Government's philosophy that decision-making, particularly where the use of economic resources is concerned, must be consciously informed by planning procedures. That is why I have taken the deliberate step of incorporating a planning function in the middle of the Department's affairs by creating a Planning Branch.

Of course there has been piecemeal planning in education before. Both in building programmes and in teacher-supply there has been planning of a kind for some years. The techniques for allocating building resources, as I said last year, have been developed throughout the post-war period; and I think we can claim it as a joint accomplishment that they are now pretty good. On the teacher-supply side we have had a number of efforts both at forecasting and planning future supply.

There has also been a remarkable improvement in educational statistics—notwithstanding the sometimes infuriating difficulties we have had in transferring some of them to the computer. I am told that this is all ultimately to the good, and that eventually our statistics will be better, as well as quicker, as a result. Meanwhile we must bear, with as much fortitude as we can, the occasional headlines in the press which accuse the Department of getting its sums wrong!

But for all these developments, we now need something more coherent and systematic in the way of education planning. We need a new framework, to which economists and sociologists as well as educationists must contribute; and this is what we shall try to develop over the next few years. It is surely inevitable that we should do so.

Just suppose for one moment (and I am speaking purely hypothetically) that all our educational spending was done by the Department. So large a sum as £1,800 millions a year would surely require the most careful planning procedures. But in fact there is not one spending agency for education, there are hundreds, and the Department itself spends only one-thirtieth of the £1,800 millions. This makes it not less but more necessary to look ahead as carefully and imaginatively as we can.

Our joint activities are a big charge on rates and taxes. We are employing (or, more strictly, you and other educational bodies are employing) a labour force approaching a million, much of it highly and therefore expensively educated. We are laying claim to a large part of the country's investment programme. Purely as a business enterprise this requires forecasting, cost-analysis, the careful relating of means to ends. I believe that for too long this large enterprise has been too haphazard, and that we need new procedures to tell us more quickly and more clearly what we are doing and what are likely to be the consequences.

But education is of course much more than just a business enterprise. Its concern is with human hopes and aspirations. When we put resources into one part rather than another we are making a judgment about social needs. Often it will be a political judgment rather than an educational judgment, because politics has to do with making choices. In the last analysis it must be the elected representatives who judge the respective claims of primary versus secondary, versus youth service, Further Education, higher education, science and so on. But when we take these decisions we must take them on the basis of the best information and analysis—educational, social, economic—that we can organize.

So there are two reasons why we have to plan educational provision: it is a large economic enterprise, and it is a large social enterprise, involving a choice of priorities. There is also

P

a third reason. Education not only uses economic resources: it also produces them. It produces educated manpower, which we know (and report after report has emphasized) is in short supply. Teachers, technologists, doctors, statisticians, scientists ... it is an imposing and growing list. Viewed from this angle the education service is perhaps the main contributor to economic growth—too important, some people say, to be left to educationists.

We therefore have to provide the educated manpower which the nation needs. Now this is not mainly a matter of detailed planning or exact forecasting. We cannot tell what precise numbers are going to be needed in five years' time in every subject or every profession or every industry—the pace of change is much too great, the demands of the future too uncertain. So we must not have the idea that the education service can, like some vast assembly line, turn out the right-sized batches of people with different kinds and degrees of education with earmarked jobs waiting for all of them. We are not moving towards that sort of society or that sort of planning. We neither want to, nor could we even if we wanted to.

True, we can identify some broad groups and some broad areas of employment, where we know we need expansion and must plan for it. Teaching is obviously one, but by no means the only one. Medicine is another, Science is another. The whole field of technology and engineering is another—and one crucial to our economic growth. And there will be others.

But apart from a few broad fields, the detailed forecasting of manpower requirements is a most uncertain business given the current pace of technological change. And this element of uncertainty argues for a high degree of flexibility in our educational system, a capacity above all to adapt to change. We know we shall need more educated manpower, but we cannot tell precisely where it will be needed. As a writer in the current *Economic Journal* puts it, 'We are always better off if we can build into the system the kind of flexibility that allows it to adjust automatically to bottlenecks and surpluses.' Unfortunately it is one of the well-known and regrettable facts about the English educational system that it develops pronounced inflexibilities.

In a recent letter to *The Times* a number of vice-chancellors developed a case which is very relevant to this issue. Even though I disagree with their case I am delighted they wrote, as nothing is more desirable than a growing dialogue between schools and universities on this sort of topic. They argued that 'a general transition to a comprehensive pattern of education' would weaken the work of sixth forms by what they called 'a diffusion of specialist staff'. Now this sounds like a positive defence of the system of early specialization which is largely forced on the schools by the requirements of university entry. But this system is surely the absolute opposite of the flexibility which we need. The extreme specialization of the English system, by which (to quote Lord Bowden) 'the whole destiny of the country is in the hands of fourteen-year-old schoolboys', has often amazed educationists from other countries. And I confess that it often amazes me—as does the assumption that it is a virtue to be defended.

For all the evidence of the country's need for a flexible labour force, particularly the highly educated part of it, points to the opposite conclusion. What is needed is not early specialization, but later specialization, not the rigidity too often imposed by university requirements, but more flexibility, not the present ridiculous system, which does untold harm to the country, under which, for example, thousands of children give up mathematics at fifteen, but a much higher degree of adaptability.

And when these vice-chancellors talk of the 'diffusion of specialist staff', what sort of sixth form do they have in mind? They sound as if they are thinking solely of the traditional type of sixth form, and sixth form curriculum, which best meets the current requirements of university entrance. But surely this is to take altogether too narrow a view of the role of the sixth form, which even in grammar schools has now begun to change quite radically. The need today is to cater both for academically

P*

inclined young people and for the increasing numbers who will be staying on into the sixth form, with perhaps no intention of going on to university, but not for that reason a negligible national asset. Indeed, it is an asset which we have largely wasted in the past by denying to so large a proportion of our children the opportunity for sixth form work.

As to the size of sixth forms, and the affects of reorganization on them, these vice-chancellors are surely taking an unduly simplified and one-sided view. This is a matter which of course we watch most carefully when we examine schemes of re-organization. But we must remember on the one hand the large number of small existing grammar schools—often two- or three-form entry—with small sixth forms and a limited range of choice, and on the other hand we must consider the large new comprehensive schools with a wider band of subjects than many grammar schools could possibly attempt. We must con-sider the possibility that with more pupils staying on to the sixth form, one large or two moderate-sized comprehensive schools may be able to replace the traditional pattern of one grammar and three secondary modern schools. We must consider also the untried but promising scope for the develop-ment of sixth form colleges in some other areas, to cater either particularly for the academic stream or for the whole range of ability; I have already approved sixteen such colleges, and have several more before me now. We must remember again the scope for transfer of sixth formers from one school to another where not every subject can be provided in every school. And we must note that reorganization is already throwing up a number of proposals for joint courses between schools and col-leges of further education. Is it not likely that we may get a better and more flexible sixth form provision under these new arrangements? And might not the universities help us to adapt to these exciting changes in school provision, instead of asking the schools to adapt to their traditional entrance requirements?

One other point about these changes. Of course there are

fewer subject specialists for sixth form teaching than we would like, especially in science and mathematics. This problem long pre-dated reorganization, and is partly due to the fact that universities retain (or even attract from the schools) so large a proportion of the graduate force.

But there is no evidence for the view of these vice-chancellors that re-organization will make this problem worse—quite the contrary. I believe that the head of an English department, who also wrote to *The Times* saying that teaching the whole ability range in a comprehensive school was 'stimulating, indeed invaluable', is representative of many young graduates coming into the schools today. And I find encouraging, the verdict of the director of the London University Institute of Education, that 'there is a striking tendency for those who do best in their training to opt for comprehensive schools.'

The price of rigidity is that errors are more disastrous—educationally for the individual, economically because they impede adaptability to technological and industrial progress. The object of manpower planning is not to lay down innumerable exact targets, but to ease our way out of traditional rigidities. It is to plan for more, not fewer, options, and to keep the choices open as long as we can.

Educational planning will not usher in a utopia in which the computer gives us all the answers, we never take a wrong decision, and nobody ever gets hurt. It is not going to be at all like that. But it should nevertheless help us in our present situation. This is a situation where standards are steadily rising —buildings are getting better, class-sizes are coming down, the level of attainment of school-leavers is rising, more and more are going into higher education.

We shall of course continue under pressure; and so we have to balance our priorities, to weigh, for example, expenditure on the socially-deprived in downtown schools against expenditure on the most able in the universities.

But no priority is ever absolute. We cannot, as some critics seem to suggest, wholly give up some things, in order to concentrate on others. We cannot sacrifice Plowden to Universities, or vice versa. This year's primary schoolchild is the undergraduate of 1977. Today's undergraduate is tomorrow's teacher. Every age-group must receive its due share of money and attention; we must advance on every front at once. This may involve a strain on our resources; but that is a permanent characteristic of any ambitious and progressive society.

So it is an illusion to suppose that planning can, or should, lay down a system of absolute priorities. What it involves is choices at the margin—not *nothing* here and everything there, but a little more here and a little less there; not everything for Plowden and nothing for Further Education, but an adjustment between many conflicting claims. The object of educational planning, which this Government has adopted for the first time in our history, is to ensure that these choices take the fullest account of all the educational and economic factors involved. It will not spirit away the problem of choices and priorities; it will enable us to make more rational choices. If it does that, it will have been abundantly justified.

Part Five
Industrial Policy

19 Monopolies and Mergers

Compiled from extracts of three speeches delivered during 1969; at Manchester on February 28th, in the House of Commons on April 17th and in London on June 25th.

I want to talk to-day about what the press have called the 'Merger Movement' — the exceptionally rapid spate of mergers which we have witnessed in the last year or two. This is an extraordinarily complex subject, which has aroused strong emotions and a lively, though sometimes rather confused, public debate.

Let us first take stock, and see where the argument now stands and what are the questions we need to answer next. I start with a few facts. The total value of company acquisitions in Britain as recently as 1964 was £501 millions; in 1968 it was £1,653 millions. In 1966, 58 mergers fell within the categories requiring examination by the Board of Trade; in 1968, 119 did so. The average size of firm being taken over is rising. The degree of concentration in British industry is certainly increasing; and mergers are playing a growing part, for good or ill, in changing the structure of industry — a part perhaps comparable in importance with the more traditional modes of internal growth and new investment.

The same trend is evident in the United States, where the total value of assets acquired by mergers rose threefold between 1966 and 1968. It is interesting that in 1968 conglomerate mergers as there defined accounted for 89 per cent of the value of all large acquisitions; while of all investment in mining and manufacturing in 1968, 45 per cent consisted of acquired assets as against internal new investment, compared with around 10 per cent ten years ago.

So I start with the proposition that large-scale mergers must be a matter of public interest and concern—that, indeed, was why Parliament passed the 1965 Monopolies and Mergers Act. They raise profound political and social, as well as economic, issues. A very large firm has a pervasive influence on people's lives. It provides the means of livelihood for many thousands of workers; its products may enter millions of homes.

For example, the reorganization that often follows a large merger may mean the closure of entire plants, with heavy redundancies. This may well be in the country's long-term economic interest. But it may cause at least temporary distress and upheaval to a large number of individuals. This is why the Department of Employment and Productivity have laid down a Code of Conduct for handling redundancy problems, under which consultation is required with the trade unions and the relevant Government Departments.

Indeed, large-scale mergers may have profound implications for the prosperity of whole towns, cities and even regions. The larger a company is, the larger each of its divisions is, and the more likely it becomes that they will be a major provider of employment in particular areas. The considerations which lead a large company to build a new plant, or close an old one, in one place rather than another, are not the same as will lead the Government to promote industrial development here and discourage it there. This is just one example of how the private and social costs of a large firm's decisions can diverge. It shows why the Government may need to obtain assurances from merging firms before allowing the merger to proceed.

Again, the actual process by which two companies merge may also raise questions of importance to the public interest. Firstly, takeover bids often lead to large capital gains for some shareholders which certainly do not make a prices and incomes policy any easier. Secondly, some of the tactics used in making or resisting some recent takeover bids have aroused criticism for discriminating between shareholders or denying some of them the opportunity of freely accepting or rejecting the bid. Hence the recent discussions of a new takeover Code and Panel.

I turn from these social arguments to the main economic argument—are mergers generally good or bad for economic efficiency? Here one confronts at once the impossibility of generalization. One can lay down certain principles—they are good if they lead to better management or greater economies of scale, bad if they lead to inertia, a dangerous lack of competition or an abuse of market power. The difficulty comes in applying these general concepts to particular industrial situations and in striking the right balance between them.

For example, the advantages conferred by size vary enormously from industry to industry. By far the majority of the computers made in the world are made by a single American company; and the number of British computer firms has been reduced to one in order to achieve the required scale of operation. In other industries—aerospace, vehicles, steel, chemicals—only really large companies can benefit in full from the economies of scale available. But in other industries the advantages of great size are much less apparent, and a small efficient company is often the pace-setter with its larger rivals trailing behind.

Again, the threat to competition from large firms depends on the size of the market. Where the market is large enough to accommodate several producers, it is possible to enjoy the economies of scale without sacrificing competition. This is one of the main advantages of trading arrangements like EFTA which in effect enlarge our home market.

So only a simpleton will come out dogmatically for or against mergers. But one has to attempt some general assessment, related to the present industrial structure of the country, of the merits of the recent merger movement; and my own firm judgment is, that it has been, on balance, beneficial. In general, mergers are desirable if they lead to better management or genuine economies of scale without eliminating workable competition. In my view, more often than not, in Britain mergers will fulfil this condition. There are still many examples of poor and out-of-date management in British industry; and many of the older industries are still too fragmented, with companies, and factories, which are too small by present-day international standards. In such industries there is clearly a need for restructuring and rationalization. And even in newer industries British companies are much smaller than their international competitors.

This is why the Government has often intervened positively to promote rationalization. This was one of the main arguments for bringing the steel industry into public ownership. I hope that my review of the structure of the textile industry, which I announced earlier this month, will lead to the organization of this industry too, in a pattern suited to the present-day demands of international competition. We have also established and encouraged the Industrial Reorganization Corporation, which is doing an excellent job in restructuring many sectors of British industry.

It is because we accept that the majority of mergers have a neutral or a beneficial effect that the Board of Trade have used so sparingly their power to refer certain mergers to the Monopolies Commission. Out of over three hundred mergers which we have examined since the 1965 Act, only ten (leaving aside two newspaper mergers which we were obliged by the legislation to refer) have in fact been referred. And in only three cases have the Commission recommended that a merger should not be allowed to proceed.

So in general the merger movement has brought clear benefits. But this does not mean that we can be uncritical and should exercise no supervision. Individual mergers may still be proposed which would not necessarily be in the public interest. For example, although very large companies may often be necessary if they are to be fully competitive in international markets, size in itself is not necessarily an advantage. Indeed, there is sometimes a risk that companies formed by mergers may become so large that any economies of scale in respect of production may be more than offset by the high costs that arise from the decline in management flexibility and control. After all, it is not difficult to think of giant companies, both in this country and elsewhere, which have proved to be sleepy and inefficient and which have found it increasingly hard to compete with small specialized companies. Moreover, great size must bring with it great financial and market power, and so greater power over employees, customers, competitors and the local community, and the risk that this power may be misused.

The conglomerate mergers, which have been in the news recently, raise rather special issues. Since the firms concerned have largely unrelated interests, questions of monopoly in the normal sense seldom arise, although a large conglomerate has it in its power to concentrate its financial resources on a small sector of industry and wield an influence out of all proportion to its market share. The sort of points which do need examining include whether top management can possibly keep a proper grip on all the new group's different activities; whether unprofitable activities will be continued too long, subsidized by profitable ones; whether there will be sufficient economies in management and finance to outweigh these dangers; whether, on the other hand, the steady advance of a skilfully run conglomerate into new fields of activity may not inject new life and efficiency into industries where competition has long since ceased to be really effective.

But the doubts which we sometimes have about a proposed merger usually arise because it will lead to a greater degree of monopoly. We are concerned here partly with the familiar dangers of monopoly—exploitation of customers by high prices; the use of financial power against inconvenient competitors, even to the extent of taking them over; exclusive dealing; discriminatory pricing; and other means of keeping competitors out. The Monopolies Commission's reports provide many examples of this kind of behaviour. But perhaps more serious is the effect which insulation from competitive pressures can have on a firm's efficiency. It can easily slip back into inertia and slackness, have no incentive to take risks, to invest in the latest methods or to satisfy new and changing consumer tastes. As Professor Hicks once put it, 'The greatest of all monopoly profits may be a quiet life!' Sometimes the market is only large enough for one firm and these risks have to be taken; moreover if there is keen competition from imports the dangers of domestic monopoly will clearly be less. But in many cases they do exist, and this is why it is necessary to have the Monopolies Commission there to safeguard competition.

It will be clear from what I have said that the complexity and variety of the issues place great demands on the understanding and judgment of the Commission. The final decision is mine, but I must rely heavily on the Commission for fact-finding, analysis and assessment. A great deal hangs on their decisions, which can affect the efficiency of British commerce and industry for years to come. I regard it as vitally important that the members of the Commission should be people of great ability and distinction—in industry, commerce, finance, law, academic life, public service—who can focus on these problems a wealth of combined experience. I shall very shortly announce the appointment of a number of new members who will, I am sure, help to preserve and enhance the high standard of the Commission's work.

I am particularly anxious to maintain a strong Commission because there seems to me a danger that mergers may become too much of a fashion. There have been signs recently of 'merger fever', which may lead to ill-considered unions and a disproportionate expense of time and energy by top management in plotting and resisting takeover bids. The existence of the powers in the 1965 Act, and the known willingness of the Government to use them, can provide just a sufficient restraining influence.

There is no inconsistency in this attitude of saying that most mergers are acceptable and even beneficial, but that a few are not. Situations differ in different industries and call for different

remedies. Where firms are too small, they should be permitted
and even encouraged to merge. If the unaided working of market forces will not bring this about in time, the Government
may need to intervene to promote it. But where we think that
a merger may lead to monopoly power, without a compensating gain in efficiency, it is right that a thorough investigation
should be made. There is thus no conflict between the Government's policies in promoting rationalization and in keeping a
check on monopolies and mergers. They are complementary
aspects of our wider policy of inducing the best allocation of
resources and the largest improvements in efficiency.

Finally, I want to deal with a question which has been raised
in recent public discussion, and to which I have given a great
deal of thought. Are our decisions, to refer Merger A but not
Merger B, consistent? And assuming that they are, should we
not publish some public criteria or guidelines, on the United
States model, which will give industry some sense of certainty?

I am sure that our decisions are consistent. In each case we
examine the likely effect of a merger on the structure of the
market—how far competition will disappear; how much will
remain; ease of entry; the countervailing power of suppliers
and customers; the availability of substitutes. We see whether
there are any broader plans for reorganizing the industry and,
if so, whether the proposed merger is consistent with them.
We look for any undue accumulation of economic power, or
concentration of managerial decision-taking. On the other side
we weigh the prospects of economies of scale, of more effective
use of assets, of rationalization in finance and marketing. We
consider any foreseeable effect on the balance of payments and
on the ability and incentive to innovate. We take account of
the likely effects on employment prospects and the distribution
of industry, comparing these, not with the situation today, but
with what might happen if the merger did not take place. These
are the questions we ask about every merger we consider. The
answers vary according to the circumstances of each case, but
the method and approach are the same.

But should we publish general guidelines, or at least give reasons in particular cases? So far the general view in Britain has been that we should not. Firstly, this would go counter to the philosophy of all our post-war monopolies legislation which, in contrast to the anti-trust philosophy of the United States, does not start from the assumption that certain types of market structure and behaviour are undesirable in themselves. Successive Governments have taken the view that we must re-tain complete freedom to judge, in each individual case, what benefits and detriments there might be, and what factors might or might not be relevant. Thus the 1965 Act on mergers, reflecting this agreed philosophy, gives the Board of Trade absolute discretion, and neither lays down guidelines itself nor requires the Board to do so.

Secondly, it is difficult to lay down guidelines which are not either so platitudinous as to be useless (for example that higher exports are 'good' or that the elimination of competition is 'bad'), or so rigid or inflexible as to stop many desirable mergers. For example, the American guidelines are extremely rigid about permissible shares of the market. When considering whether to challenge a merger between competitors, they first of all classify the market as 'highly concentrated', 'less highly concentrated' or 'has a trend towards concentration'. Each category has its own complex set of rules based on market shares. For example, in a 'highly concentrated' market situa-tion—one in which the shares of the four largest firms amount to approximately 75 per cent or more, the Department of Justice have said that they will ordinarily challenge mergers where the acquiring firm has 4 per cent of the market and the other firm has 4 per cent or more; or where the acquiring firm has 10 per cent of the market and the other 2 per cent or more. If the acquiring firm has 15 per cent or more, then the acqui-sition of a competitor with 1 per cent or more is likely to be challenged. Now in a huge economy like the United States, where large size is easily attained without loss of competition, this sort of arithmetic is acceptable. But in a smaller economy like ours, where necessary size may inevitably mean a certain degree of monopoly, such an approach could be very damaging in relation to international competition.

If we were to take the American guidelines as a model, what would happen? We should specify the market share which would lead us to make a reference to the Commission; for example, we should refer all mergers where the market share of the combined companies exceeded, say, 50 per cent. We should also have to specify the size of mergers which would be referred to the Commission; for example, if the assets of the two companies together exceeded, say, £100 millions. On conglomerates, we could not follow the American guidelines, since they are not at all specific. We should have to formulate our own exact definition of conglomerates and lay down, for example, that any conglomerate so defined involving over, say, £50 millions of assets would be referred. Also, to reduce uncertainty we should have to say, as is done in the United States, that in the cases we had specified a reference to the Commission would be automatic and despite any benefits which might be claimed from the merger. Otherwise, we should be back to the same position as we are in today.

I am quite clear that, however suitable such guidelines may be in the United States, they would not do here. To adopt them would, to begin with, involve major legislation which overthrew the whole basis of all our post-war monopoly legislation under successive Governments, for this does not start from the assumption that certain types of market structure are undesirable in themselves. On the contrary, it adopts an entirely empirical and pragmatic approach.

Quite apart from the legislative side of the question, such guidelines would be highly unwelcome to British industry. They would fit badly with our policy, which I am sure is correct, of encouraging desirable mergers through the I.R.C. They would involve referring a far higher proportion of mergers to the Commission. They would impose a degree of rigidity which would make no sense in a country so heavily dependent on international trade and so subject to international competition as we are in Britain. It is not even clear that they would eliminate uncertainty. In difficult cases, American-style guidelines leave a lot of room for argument on interpretation. For example, how do we define the relevant geographical and industrial markets, particularly in a country like ours which imports as much as we do? It seems likely to me, having thought about this a great deal, that the merger cases which cause most difficulty under our present system would cause at least as much difficulty if we were to adopt arithmetical guidelines on the American pattern.

The fact is that the use of guidelines in the United States is related to an entirely different legislative philosophy, different institutional arrangements, and a different international trade situation. Their legislation prohibits any steps which might lead to a significant reduction in competition, with the result that a large proportion of important mergers are manifestly unlawful. For all the reasons that I have given, I believe that this would not be the right policy for this country.

Nor would it do us any good to adopt guidelines without the arithmetical criteria, because then the guidelines would be either meaningless or totally platitudinous, consisting of saying that more exports are good or that exploitation of the consumer is bad. They would be liable to endlessly different interpretations. They would in no way increase the certainty of the business community as to when we were likely to refer and when not. Yet they might inhibit the freedom of action which the 1965 Act was intended to give us, so I think that we would probably get the worst of both worlds.

However, within the framework of the present legislation, I should like to give more information about the way we deal with mergers and more explanation of how we use the discretion which the law confers on us, but without attempting to formulate guidelines as such. I want to do this for three reasons: to assist informed discussion, to help firms prepare themselves when they have to present merger cases to the

Board of Trade, and to show, as I believe to be the case, that we are following a consistent attitude. But we must do it without tying ourselves to rigid or detailed rules and without running any risk of distorting industry's rationalization plans to fit some non-existent notion of an 'ideal' merger.

I have decided to issue later this year a concise but comprehensive publication, on the subject.[1] I want it to provide, both for those who are directly concerned in merger questions and also for the interested public, extensive information about the Government's attitude and practices in this sphere. Without laying down rules, it will explain our procedures in merger cases. It will describe the questions which we ask of merging firms and the factors that we take into account in deciding whether or not to make a reference to the Commission.

Of course, the weight that we attach to the different factors must vary with the individual circumstances of the particular case, and the final decision must depend on a balance of considerations. But I hope that this publication, besides explaining our procedures in a way which will be useful to industry, and, I hope, interesting to public opinion, will also show that our criteria and approach to mergers are consistent, and consistent, too, with other aspects of the Government's industrial policy, such as support for the I.R.C.

There is one other change of emphasis which I want to make, and it concerns assurances from merging firms. After all, the choice is not simply whether to refer a merger to the Commission or not. There may be good reasons for not referring a merger because the advantages to be expected from it are, on balance, clear ones, and yet one may want to obtain from the companies concerned some assurances as to future behaviour. Alternatively, it may be unnecessary to refer a merger, where one simple, obvious disadvantage can be identified, if this can be dealt with by a firm assurance. For example, as the House knows, one of the anxieties which I felt about the E.M.I./ A.B.P.C. merger was met by an assurance that E.M.I. would divest itself of its talent agency. There are other cases in which

I have approved a merger, only after receiving similar assurances, the latest being Ross and Associated Fisheries, where I thought that the merger on balance was clearly desirable, but was most anxious to safeguard the position of the merchanting side of the industry.

I do not propose to ask for assurances in every single case, because the fact is that the great majority of mergers are relatively small-scale affairs, neither obviously very good nor obviously very bad, and not raising problems to which assurances are relevant. But I propose in future to seek assurances somewhat more freely in major merger cases. For example, in co-operation with my Right Hon. Friend the First Secretary, I want assurances about the handling, by the companies concerned, of the problems of industrial relations to which rationalization and redundancy may give rise. Rationalization is often desirable, but it can be very painful to the workers and families involved. It must be carried through in proper consultation with the unions concerned and without unnecessary or avoidable injury to the interests of the workers affected.

Again, in large-scale mergers I must see and be assured that proper attention is paid to the Government's regional policies. In other cases, particularly in the case of a takeover bid from overseas, I may need to be assured that exports will not be prejudiced nor imports unreasonably increased. Lastly, there are the specific assurances related to the particular circumstances of the industry which I may seek in such cases as E.M.I. or Ross/Associated Fisheries, which I have already quoted. These assurances will never form a major part of our monopolies and mergers policy, but they can represent one useful step towards the accountability of large firms which we on this side of the House have always wanted.

I hope that these changes of emphasis, while preserving the flexibility in our approach which I think has the support of both sides of the House, will give the public a greater sense both of certainty and of consistency.

Getting the right industrial structure, of course, is only part of the whole problem of achieving a better export performance and a general improvement in competitiveness. That, at the end of the day, is what all the problems are about and what determines our standard of living. If we want to improve that standard of living, it is towards improving our industrial competitiveness that the efforts of us all, whether Government, management or unions, must be concentrated.

20 *Government and Industry*

Address to the Trade Union Public Services International, Copenhagen, September 1971.

The most fundamental question concerning the distribution of national income is not necessarily the distribution of income to various groups but the question of the growth of Gross National Product, because without a dynamic growth-rate there cannot really be significant redistribution.

The fact that a healthy growth-rate exists does not ensure redistribution of incomes; this depends largely on political factors and the social values a particular government holds. But a slow growth-rate, at least, rules out significant redistribution. The reason is a simple one; that if the economy as a whole is scarcely growing, then a redistribution of income to some particular group, must mean that the incomes of the rest of the population will suffer not merely a relative decline but an absolute decline. In the rough democratic world we live in, we shall not get a major redistribution of income in the direction we want unless we have rapid and sustained economic growth.

Perhaps I could illustrate this by putting it in another way: if we want substantially more money for public service employees this will normally mean higher government expenditure and that, in turn, will normally mean higher taxation. Now people will never like paying taxes. We all of us want to keep more money for ourselves and our families, and quite naturally so. But people will dislike paying taxes even more if their standard of living is scarcely rising, and if the effect of higher taxes is actually to reduce their standard of living. In other words, the chance of getting more money by taxation and by higher public spending–and this is critical to what you are daily trying to do that chance is reduced in a country with a low growth-rate, and it is interesting that this proposition is strongly confirmed by a recent O.E.C.D. study which came to the conclusion, 'that the growth-rate of government spending tends to be highest in countries where the growth of output is highest'. In other words, I believe that all our hopes fundamentally depend, not just on redistributing a static income, but on achieving a sustained growth of income, and that is why the behaviour of the economy must be, and of course is, of intense concern to all trade unionists.

Now, how does one ensure a more rapid growth of the economy? The crux of the matter is of course—in the jargon of the moment—in macro-economic policy; that is, in the government so managing demand that we have full employment, that we have a favourable climate for high investment, and I would also add, to strike a more controversial note, that we have a healthy level of profits, and I refer to profits in both the public and private sectors. A little-noticed factor in Great Britain over the last ten years has been the very sharp decline in profits, both public and private, as a share of the national income. I do not believe that it is possible to attain the high investment we want if profits show so dramatic a decline. Now, managing the economy so as to maintain full employment is, as we know, perfectly feasible; governments know technically how they can do it. The great service of Keynes to recent history is that we now know, in the way that governments did not know in the 1930s, how full employment can be maintained. So the question is why is full employment not maintained the whole time? Why, in many of our countries, do we have periodic bouts of deflation, of stop-go, of the kind of unemployment that we are observing and suffering in Great Britain today, with all the loss of output, with all the waste of resources that this unemployment involves? This happens, I believe, because governments give way to the temptation of using stop-go and using deflation as their main method of controlling the economy, and in particular as their main method of dealing, number one, with balance of payments crises and, number two, with wage and price inflation. So that if we want sustained growth of the kind that, at least in some of our countries, we are currently not achieving, we must find other methods for dealing with wage and price inflation.

As far as the balance of payments is concerned, I have no doubt about what the alternative methods should be in principle. It should be a more flexible attitude to changes in exchange rates than we have had, at least until the very recent past. The Bretton Woods system, created in 1944-5, has undoubtedly done the world great service; it has enabled us to have twenty years of almost unparalleled prosperity, but it has recently become a great deal too rigid. Indeed, it has become rigid in a way that its founders, such as Keynes, never intended. Certainly in the last three to four years there has been some loosening up, with excellent results. I think most people would agree that the changes in the parities of Britain, France and Germany in the last four years brought at any rate more stability to the international economic scene. And now President Nixon's measures have, to put it mildly, loosened the system up still further. Now, we rightly have strong objections to the ten per cent surcharge and to other features of the Nixon package, but nevertheless I believe that it has done the world some service and I think that we now have the possibility of settling down to a new and far more flexible system.

As far as wage and price inflation are concerned, I have no doubts in my mind that we must have a prices and incomes policy. We must have it because the only alternative will be squeeze and deflation. Governments, if they are faced with a huge annual price inflation of seven per cent, eight per cent and nine per cent, will not endure this indefinitely. For one thing, the voters will not allow them to, and if they have no other method of dealing with inflation, they will resort to the old, old method of a harsh budget of stop-go, of deflation and unemployment. I personally, and I hope I tread on no toes here, believe that a prices and incomes policy is also necessary for reasons of social justice, and reasons of social equality. I observe that in a free-for-all what tends to happen in my country is that those who do best are the doctors, the airline pilots and the most highly paid professional groups, those who do next best are the already highly paid technicians, those who do third best are probably a group like the motor car workers, those who do fourth best are large groups of public service employees, and as to people with really low wages, they come absolutely nowhere. So I think that both on grounds of full employment and also on grounds of social justice we need such a policy, but I wholly agree with what Mr Donnet said from this rostrum earlier this morning, that such a policy is only possible within a framework of government policies for greater social and economic equality as a whole. It is no good simply asking the trade unions to cooperate in a prices and incomes policy against a background of reactionary social policies.

Now, so much briefly for what I called 'the macro-economic' side of policy, the need to ensure full employment and sustained growth. I now turn to what may be done as far as particular pressures are concerned. There are, to begin with, a number of general industrial pressures which a government can use to improve the performance of the economy, pressures which frequently apply both to public and private industries. These are, for example, investment incentives to increase investment above the level which it would otherwise believe desirable, although this can lead, as it has led in my country now and again, to highly wasteful investment. Regional policies, a critical matter in a number of our countries, including my own, to make sure that certain regions, with particular historical difficulties, share in the full employment that the rest of the country is enjoying. Indicative planning, which I believe to be necessary, although I have some doubts as to how central a role it actually plays. A consistent policy for competition, monopoly and mergers, extremely important for the private sector, though I am not quite certain that any of our countries yet have a wholly consistent policy in this field. Greater financial disclosure, on the part of private industry in partiucular, for in Britain there is a marked contrast between the situation of public industry and the situation of private industry. Public industry, for example, publishes a mass of information, very long annual reports, and is subject to public investigations by the Parliamentary Select Committee on the nationalized industries. Indeed, there is very little that is not known about the performance of the nationalized industries, but the position in the private sector is wholly different, where there is still quite inadequate disclosure, particularly in the multi-product companies.

But I want to talk particularly now, not about these general pressures, which affect all industries in a country, but about specific pressures on both public and private industry, which affect a particular firm or particular industry. In other words, I want to talk about the policy which has come to be known in Britain, as selective intervention. I deliberately ignore the much wider question, which would need a whole lecture in itself, of public versus private ownership. In any case, your members for the most part are already in the public sector. I am talking of policies within the framework of our present mixed economy. The purpose of these policies is to improve the economic performance of a particular firm or particular industry, either by changing its management or by changing its structure or by leading to better and more sensible investment decisions. Such intervention will frequently be needed. The question, which is a very important question for trade unionists, is who should do this intervention, this restructuring, who should be responsible for altering the management, the structure, the performance of an industry or a firm? There are a number of possibilities. The first possibility is to have an internal warning system. If you like, an internal fail-safe mechanism against the firm, whether public or private, which is sliding downhill, unbeknown to the outside public. To take a dramatic illustration from Great Britain, the case of Rolls-Royce. Rolls-Royce was on the point of financial collapse many, many months before this became known to any outside body, including the government. Another example from Great Britain, was the example of the British Motor Company, which became merged with British Leyland. The British Motor Company was gradually sliding downhill under an incompetent management, but somehow there was no warning mechanism, there was no way of changing the situation without a huge external upheaval.

I think there are one or two possibilities of introducing such a warning system, particularly against the enterprise, whether public or private, which is effectively dominated by a single individual and this incidentally is becoming more common in my country. Instead of having a chairman and also a managing director, we frequently have only a chairman/managing director who effectively dominates his board, and this domination by an individual can be found in nationalized industry as well as in private industry. One possibility is on every board to have non-executive directors of real power and influence, not just people appointed because they retired from something else and a job was found for them, but non-executive directors with sufficient influence and sufficient public reputation such that if they saw something going wrong and subsequently resigned from the board, this would cause a big public outcry. A similar result could be obtained through the method of a supervisory board, of which one or two countries represented here have a good deal of experience. I have no panacea myself but I am sure, having observed industry for some considerable time under the Labour Government, that what is needed inside the enterprise itself is a warning system to warn the government and the public when the affairs of the enterprise are beginning a slow decline.

That is one possibility. A second possibility is an external investigation by some outside standing body. In Britain, for example, by the Parliamentary Select Committee on the nationalized industries. A third possibility is a State Holdings Agency or a body like the I.R.C. in Britain—a roving body with money of its own and a high degree of independence. This raises problems of democratic accountability, and I do not myself think that we have yet achieved the synthesis between independence on the one hand and democratic accountability on the other that we need.

The fourth obvious method of improving the structure of a firm or an industry is direct intervention by the government to change the structure or to change the management. An intervention that, of course, is particularly common in the public sector. There are some dangers about the notion of direct government intervention in the structure of a particular firm or industry. I can say that politicians, for example, are not equipped for this task and nor in my view are civil servants. Politicians are trained to be politicians and not experts in the detail of industrial structure. Civil servants are trained to be professional administrators and again not experts in industrial structure. So I have some reservations about ambitious ministers and ambitious officials just thinking they can do the job on their own successfully. There is of course a further difficulty: that if the job was left to ministers and civil servants there would inevitably be a lack of continuity due to political change. In Britain under the Labour Government there were two successive policies for the textile industry in two successive years, merely because the minister in charge of the industry had altered during those years. To take another very current case in Britain, which some of my colleagues are concerned with, the reform of local government, there is now, with the election of a Tory Government, a completely different set of reform proposals from the ones in existence only a year previously from the Labour Government.

And, of course, it is not only political change. There is a danger of too much ideology as against merit. We have in Britain at the moment, a desperate struggle taking place between the Tory Minister, Mr John Davies, and Lord Melchett, the Chairman of the British Steel Corporation, about the future structure of the steel industry, and there is no doubt in my mind that the minister's proposals initially were ideologically motivated and not based on an objective study of merits. The same is true of many of the current Tory proposals; I am happy to say that most of them look like coming to very little. Nevertheless plans have been made for denationalization and for hiving off. The two different views of the two political parties on local government reform is by no means a matter of chance or accident. The two proposals differ fundamentally, because the Labour proposals favoured the urban areas, where 80 per cent of the population in Britain lives; while the Tory proposals greatly favoured the rural areas, where many of their most vocal supporters live. The same differences are seen with the reorganization of the National Health Service.

There is one other difficulty about direct political intervention: it is often influenced by fashion, and fashion in industrial matters frequently changes. There are changing views from one decade to another about the virtues of large size as opposed to small size. There are changing views about the virtues of centralization as against the virtues of decentralization, and politicians and civil servants are particularly prone to listen to these changes in fashion. So direct government intervention sometimes produces the wrong solution. But not always; to quote another example, from Britain, I believe that the recent reform of the civil aviation industry, relying mainly on the report of the Edwards Committee,[1] has been a substantial success. The post-Fulton[2] reforms of the civil service have probably led to a marked improvement, and there are some nationalized sectors, such as transport, where I would certainly claim that recent structural changes have been very much for the better. And one has to remember that one cannot achieve a 100 per cent success when one is talking about structural changes of this character. There is no single objectively right solution in any particular case. One has to remember that private mergers are frequently a disastrous failure. So, if a government can achieve a 51 per cent success in this field it would in fact be doing very well and one needs to be reasonably modest in the views of what actually can be attained.

But in any case, and this is a point which I want to stress, whether the changes are for the better or whether they are for the worse, they will all have the most profound effect on the trade unions in the industry concerned. I believe that it is in this public service sector that it is of growing importance for the unions to form and to press strong views as to what they think to be the right industrial structure. In pressing these views, they would naturally seek to advance the principle of workers' participation, both at the level of the board, at the level of top management (where we have a lot to learn from the experience of Germany or recently in our own steel industry in Britain), and, perhaps even more important, at the shop floor level, where I believe the strongest desire for participation manifests itself.

I want to make one passing remark here. I have talked today about the industry and the enterprise in terms of performance, because the whole of what I have been saying relates to the urgent necessity to improve the performance of our economies if we are to obtain the redistribution of income which we want. But it could be that in five years or in ten years time, when we are discussing the behaviour of an industry or corporation, whether public or private, we shall not be discussing it in terms of performance. We may, by then, be following the example of the United States, where attitudes towards the corporation have varied markedly over the last half century or more. From the 1890s onwards, the days of the Sherman Act, when people spoke of the corporation in the United States they were solely interested in the question of size, and the power that that size might generate. Then fifty years later there came a period when Americans, talking about the corporation, talked solely in terms of its performance. But today in the United States, where, for most of the population though not all, there is a very high standard of living, people have now almost ceased to talk about the performance of the corporation, and they talk about the social responsibility of the corporation. They talk about its safety standards. They talk about what it does about pollution or fails to do about pollution. They talk about the ratio of non-whites that the corporation employs at different levels of management. They talk about whether or not it trades with South Africa. They talk about the whole range of consumer issues that Ralph Nader has so dramatically brought to the forefront of public attention, so that when people now demonstrate outside the doors of General Motors, they are not demonstrating about its poor or good performance, they are demonstrating about its degree of social responsibility and all this opens up a new area which, I hope, with a rising standard of living, will come to be increasingly important to us in Europe.

But I return to the question of performance and what is really my essential message today. We are living in a period of unprecedented rapid industrial change and structural change, not only in industry but also in services. These changes are going to have the most profound effect on the standard of living of your members and I believe that it is now as important that the unions should begin to take the most positive view of industrial structure and of structural change, as they have for long past taken of national economic policy. Whether one is talking about the reform in Britain of the National Health Service, or about the structure of the Electricity Supply Industry, it is crucial to have a strong trade union position which is firmly pressed on those who are carrying out the reform. This, I think, in practice, is one of the most important aspects of worker and trade union participation, and on your success in influencing this, in practice, will substantially depend the standard of living of all your members.

Notes and Sources

Chapter 1

1. *The Future of Socialism* (Jonathan Cape, London, 1956), ch. 8; Michael Young, *The Rise of the Meritocracy* (Thames and Hudson, London, 1958); *The Conservative Enemy* (Jonathan Cape, London, 1962), ch. 11; John Rawls, *A Theory of Justice* (Harvard, Cambridge, Mass., 1971).
2. Wilfred Beckerman (ed.), *The Labour Government's Economic Record 1964–70* (Duckworth, London, 1972); Peter Townsend and Nicholas Bosanquet (eds.), *Labour and Inequality* (Fabian Society, London, 1972); Michael Young and Alan Fox in their *Socialist Commentary* essays (respectively January and June 1973).
3. *Economic Trends*, October 1973.
4. *National Income and Expenditure 1973* (Blue Book, H.M.S.O., London). All further economic statistics not otherwise attributed come from this source.
5. Michael Stewart in Beckerman, op. cit., pp. 110–11.
6. I have drawn freely here on Howard Glennerster's chapter in Townsend and Bosanquet, op. cit.
7. S. M. Lipset, *The Public Interest*, Fall 1972.
8. Evidence to the House of Commons Expenditure Committee (Trade and Industry Sub-Committee), Session 1972–3.
9. Jeremy Hardie in Beckerman, op. cit.
10. *Royal Commission on the Constitution* (October 1973, Cmnd 5460 61), vol. II, Memorandum of Dissent, p. 34.
11. Dudley Jackson, H. A. Turner and Frank Wilkinson, *Do Trade Unions Cause Inflation?* (Cambridge University Press, London, 1972), p. 66.
12. Jackson, Turner and Wilkinson, op. cit.
13. S. J. Prais in *Oxford Economic Papers* (forthcoming).
14. Andrew Glyn and Bob Sutcliffe, *British Capitalism, Workers and the Profits Squeeze* (Penguin, Harmondsworth, 1972), p. 10.
15. Daniel Bell, *The Coming of Post-Industrial Society* (Basic Books, New York, 1973), ch. 2.
16. M. D. Steuer *et al.*, *The Impact of Foreign Direct Investment on the United Kingdom* (H.M.S.O., London, 1973); *Multinational Corporations in World Development* (United Nations, 1973).

17. The figures and quotations in this and the next three paragraphs are all from Steuer, op. cit.
18. United Nations, op. cit., p. 39.
19. Edmund Dell, *Political Responsibility and Industry* (Allen and Unwin, London, 1973).
20. Though often with some difficulty; C. D. Foster, *Politics, Finance and the Role of Economics* (Allen and Unwin, London, 1971).
21. Cmd. 5461, Memorandum of Dissent, pp. 30 seq.
22. Arthur Lewis, *Socialism and Economic Growth* (London School of Economics, 1971), pp. 11–12.
23. *Industrial Review to 1977* (National Economic Development Office, 1973).
24. Richard Pryke, *Public Enterprise in Practice* (MacGibbon and Kee, London, 1971), p. 442.
25. *The Responsibilities of the British Public Company* (C.B.I., 1973).
26. *Management in a Changing Society* (B.I.M., 1973).
27. *The Conservative Enemy*, pp. 90–91.
28. H. A. B. Atkinson, *Unequal Shares* (Allen Lane, London, 1972), ch. 9; *Capital and Equality* (Labour Party, 1973).
29. For we have to remember that production-line workers make up only a comparatively small proportion of the population.
30. W. E. J. McCarthy and N. D. Ellis, *Management by Agreement* (Hutchinson, London, 1973).
31. *Industrial Democracy* (T.U.C., 1973).
32. Also in the U.S., where the Lemberg Centre for the Study of Violence has reported a dramatic fall in the amount of group violence and civil disturbance in the last five years.
33. *Labour and the Economy: a Socialist Strategy* (Fabian Tract 413, May 1972).

Chapter 4
1. John Gyford and Stephen Haseler, *Social Democracy: Beyond Revisionism* Fabian Society, London, 1971).
2. D. E. Butler and M. Pinto-Duschinsky, *The British General Election of 1970* (Macmillan, London, 1971).

Chapter 6
1. Colin Buchanan and Partners, *The Prospect for Housing* (A study for the Nationwide Building Society, London, 1971).
2. See above, p. 71.

Chapter 7
1. Fabian Research Series, No. 297 (1971).

Chapter 8
1. Peter Townsend and Nicholas Bosanquet (eds.), op. cit.
2. Wilfrid Beckerman (ed.), op. cit.

Chapter 10
1. *The Grief Report* (Shelter, 1972).

Chapter 11
1. *Report to the Minister of Housing and Local Government on Proposals for the Transfer of G.L.C. Housing to the London Boroughs* (October 1970), 2 vols.
2. John Greve, *Homelessness in London* (Scottish Academic Press, Edinburgh, 1971).
3. Since published as *Greater London Development Plan: Report of the Panel of Inquiry* (H.M.S.O., London, 1973), 2 vols.

Chapter 12
1. *Progress Report on Fight Against Pollution* (May 27th, 1970, Cmnd. 4373).

Chapter 13
1. Minority report in *Commission on the Third London Airport* (H.M.S.O., 1971).
2. STOL – Short Take-off and Landing
   VTOL – Vertical Take-off and Landing

Chapter 14
1. *Greater London Development Plan* (G.L.C., 1969), 2 vols.
2. *Greater London Development Plan: Report of the Panel of Inquiry.*

Chapter 15
1. *Report of the Royal Commission on Local Government in England and Wales* (June 1969, Cmnd. 4040).
2. *Report of Local Authority and Allied Personal Services* (July 1968, Cmnd. 3703).

Chapter 16
1. *Early Leaving, Report of the Central Advisory Council for Education (England)* (H.M.S.O., London, 1955).
2. J. E. Floud, A. H. Halsey and F. M. Martin, *Social Class and Educational Opportunity* (1956).
3. P. E. Vernon (ed.), *Secondary School Selection* (1957).

4. *Report of the Committee on Higher Education* (October 1965, Cmnd. 2154).
5. J. W. B. Douglas, *The Home and the School* (1964).

Chapter 17
1. *Report of the Committee on Higher Education* (October 1963, Cmnd. 2154).
2. Speech made at Woolwich Polytechnic, April 27th, 1965.
3. *Report of the Study Group on the Government of Colleges of Education* (H.M.S.O., London, 1966).

Chapter 18
1. Cmnd. 3291, 1967.

Chapter 19
1. *Mergers: A Guide to Board of Trade Practice* (H.M.S.O., London 1969).

Chapter 20
1. *Report of the Civil Air Transport Committee* (May 1969, Cmnd. 4018).
2. *Report of the Committee on the Civil Service* (June 1968, Cmnd. 3638).